# THE SUPER-
# INTENDENCY
# IN THE
# NINETIES

**M. William Konnert, Ed. D.**
Kent State University

**John J. Augenstein, Ph. D.**
Marquette University

# THE SUPER-INTENDENCY IN THE NINETIES

## WHAT SUPERINTENDENTS AND BOARD MEMBERS NEED TO KNOW

**TECHNOMIC**
PUBLISHING CO., INC.

LANCASTER · BASEL

# The Superintendency in the Nineties

a TECHNOMIC® publication

*Published in the Western Hemisphere by*
Technomic Publishing Company, Inc.
851 New Holland Avenue
Box 3535
Lancaster, Pennsylvania 17604 U.S.A.

*Distributed in the Rest of the World by*
Technomic Publishing AG

Printed in the United States of America
10  9  8  7  6  5  4  3  2  1

Main entry under title:
  The Superintendency in the Nineties: What Superintendents and Board Members
    Need to Know

A Technomic Publishing Company book
Bibliography: p.
Index p. 239

Library of Congress Card No. 90-70986
ISBN No. 87762-757-6

# CONTENTS

**PART TWO: THE SUPERINTENDENT AS LEADER**

Leadership Subsection A—The Broader Leadership Perspective

Leadership Subsection B—Personal Philosophy and Leadership

# FOREWORD

America has been busily reforming its public schools—toward teacher professionalism, school-site management, parental involvement, and effective principaling. Mysteriously lost in much of the improve-the-schools discussion has been a consideration of the impact of local education's chief executive officer: the school district superintendent. This, despite predictions that upwards of three-quarters of all U.S. superintendents will be eligible to retire by 1994.

M. William Konnert and John Augenstein provide herein a timely, down-to-earth, and eminently useful treatment of the local superintendency. By no means is this a how-to-do-it book. It has much substance—with a solid theoretical and/or historical examination of superintendents' leadership, school board/superintendent relations, and the array of duties/demands upon the superintendency. Nevertheless, the authors are also refreshingly practical. The *do's-and-don'ts* of effective school board relations, use of outside consultants, and the superintendent's participation in collective bargaining and legislative lobbying are among the topics liberally sprinkled with *tips* for the practicing administrator. The authors also include some seldom-addressed suggestions for preparing for, obtaining, and remaining healthy in this stress-filled profession. Furthermore, the book is much strengthened through the authors' collaboration with an array of practicing school administrators in the initial preparation of nearly every substantive chapter.

Two developments are likely to shape mightily the course of the superintendency in the 1990s. Konnert and Augenstein give thorough attention to both. The first is a continued politicization of the role of local education's chief executive officer, with an accompanying demand for exceptional skills in communication, negotiation, and conflict resolution. Learning to take criticism and simultaneously a willingness to take risks are just two of many *political* qualities of modern-day administration that have not been easily acquired attributes of local superintendents. Similarly, as a second development of the 1990s, any remaining images of the superintendent as a take-charge, from-the-top-down, near-autocratic leader of local education will have long disappeared. The authors correctly picture the local superintendent working hard to shape organizational values rather than issuing directives and empowering others rather than prescribing roles and procedures. This, as advertised, is a book for the 1990s in school administration, and a book which should appeal to both *old hand* and *rookie* alike.

Robert L. Crowson
Professor of Educational Administration
The University of Illinois at Chicago

## INTRODUCTION

This book addresses the unique position in the school systems of the United States known as the superintendency, and the individual, known as the superintendent, who occupies this position. This individual is the chief executive officer (CEO) of the school system. As such, the superintendent has no peers within the school system and is *the* leader of the system. The occupant of this position must possess a sense of vision of what the system can be and have a view of the system that is broad in its perspective and thus, different than anyone else's. The superintendency is more than knowing *how to do*, it is knowing *how to think* and *how to feel*.

The traditionally accepted definition of the superintendent as the implementer of policy established by the board of education is far too simplistic. The reality of the situation is that a dynamic and ever changing relationship exists between the superintendent and a host of people and agencies including such publics as parents, community groups, students, school personnel, and state and federal agencies. The superintendent at different times and in different situations is a leader, coach, manager, follower, motivator, philosopher, missionary, policy maker, politician, sales person, evaluator, and distributor of scarce resources. The degree to which this individual is able to establish a value system and mission for the school district and persuade others to share these commitments and be motivated to work toward their attainment, determines superintendency success.

The basic purposes of this book are to provide information that will help individuals prepare for, obtain, and be successful in their first superintendency and to help practicing superintendents improve their CEO skills. The size, demographics, or geographic location of the school system do little to alter the primary responsibilities of the position.

The book is divided into four parts. An overview of each part follows.

## PART ONE (The Milieu of the Superintendent)

We feel that an overall perspective and understanding of the setting in which the superintendent functions is a prerequisite to studying and understanding the superintendency. Part one begins with a brief history of the superintendency. This is important, for organizational research indicates that the history of an organization has a meaningful influence on the current state of affairs within the organization.

Following the historical perspective, the contemporary setting for the superintendency is explored from a *macro* or *big picture* perspective. This exploration is followed by a discussion of organizational dynamics at play within a school system. The contemporary scene concludes with a view of the school system as a political system.

Part one then moves to a discussion of the role of the superintendent in the nineties, because important changes are on the horizon. There is evidence that the superintendent is emerging as more of a mentor and coach than an order giver. There is a shift away from a hierarchical authoritarian organization to a more horizontal organization where people experience more ownership, both literal and psychological, and where they can experience personal growth. Individuals are becoming more concerned with how their work relates to the rest of their lives, and this attitude represents an increased emphasis on individual concern for the quality of life, including work life.

One other important change that presently is occurring and, in all likelihood, will continue throughout the nineties is a focus on women in educational administration. With respect to the superintendency, female superintendents currently are few in number. However, with each passing year, their numbers continue to increase. There is every reason to believe that this trend will gain in momentum during the next decade. One finds an increasing number of articles in the literature related to this topic. Charol Shakeshaft of Hofstra University published a book entitled *Women in Educational Administration* that has become a basic research source, and Colleen Bell and Susan Chase at the University of Tulsa have been pursuing research on female superintendents. These are but two examples of a growing number of individuals who have a major professional interest in the study of female administrators.

This book has been written in an effort to provide useful insights for any superintendency aspirant or incumbent, regardless of gender. In an effort to convey this message, the authors have used inclusive or nonsexist language throughout the text and have included female superintendents as contributors.

## PART TWO (The Superintendent as a Leader)

As the most extensive part of the book, this section discusses the superintendent as *the leader* of the school system. For the sake of clarity, it is presented in four subsections.

### The Broader Leadership Perspective

In order to establish a common understanding of *leadership*, this subsection presents a brief history of leadership that is followed by a discussion of the differences between providing leadership from the superintendent's chair and from other positions within the system. The superintendent must constantly be thinking about the *big issues*, and how they will be addressed without violating personal philosophical commitments. For example, the United States has entered into an information age, and the time is rapidly approaching, if not already here, when the touch of a couple of keys on a computer keyboard can *pull up* any information or facts one desires. In fact, computers can continuously and simultaneously monitor a number of information providing networks and compile a bank of relevant information in very short order. This development has tremendous implications for the mission of education for most of what is taught in the schools is factual in nature. If one can obtain facts at will by mechanical means, then what facts are still worthy of being taught in the schools?

### Personal Philosophy and Leadership

This subsection addresses the important role one's personal philosophy plays in providing leadership to the school system. Before the superintendent can select an orientation and mission for the school system, a well-established personal value system must first be in place. Further, it is necessary to know how one's personal value system applies to the education of individuals from birth through early adulthood. In short, the superintendent must have a consistent, comprehensive, and workable personal philosophy, must know how this personal philosophy influences education, and must clearly communicate these beliefs to all publics. The concept of transformational leadership and the importance of system culture and values are also explored.

## Superintendent Leadership Competencies: Personal

This subsection identifies desirable personal leadership competencies. These competencies are necessary but not sufficient attributes for general leadership success. In and of themselves they do not guarantee leadership success; however, success will be difficult to obtain without them. The superintendent is viewed as a divergent thinker, motivator, assessor and modifier of risk-taking propensity, and empowerer.

## Superintendent Leadership Competencies: Professional

This final leadership subsection identifies and discusses some important professional competencies a successful superintendent must possess. These competencies are addressed specifically from the perspective of the superintendency. The superintendent as the board's chief executive officer is the first topic addressed. This may be the most important topic with respect to the survival of the superintendent. Second, is the superintendent as negotiator. Probably nothing has a greater impact on the day-to-day working life of the superintendent than the negotiated contract and the process which led to the contract. Third, is the superintendent as communicator. Both internal and external publics are addressed. Some special areas such as communicating with the community, parents, media, special interest groups, and the *crazies* are touched upon. The section concludes with chapters on the superintendent as business manager, lobbyist, and consulter of specialists.

## A Final Leadership Comment

Conspicuously missing from the leadership subdivision is any mention of effective instructional leadership. The reason for this omission is quite simply that the entire leadership part, indeed the entire book, is about effective instructional leadership.

In a research report published by the U.S. Office of Education (1986), evidence is presented which indicates that schools with high student achievement have instructional leaders that exhibit attributes of clear and consistent decision making, fairness, and concern for a safe orderly environment. One could make a case that these are attributes that would be important in any organizational setting.

Quality instructional leadership is the effective application of leadership to an educational setting. This is the essence of the book. To be an effective leader in a school system is to be an effective instructional leader. The two cannot be separated.

The study of leadership is exciting in part because it is so elusive. Long (1988, p. 21) expresses this elusiveness well when he states:

> Analyzing leadership . . . is like studying the Abominable Snowman: you see footprints, but never the thing itself. Leadership is like electricity. You can't see it, but you certainly can't miss its effect. And yet, this elusive, intangible thing we call leadership might very well be the most essential ingredient in personal and business success.

## PART THREE (Preparing for, Obtaining, and Departing a Superintendency)

This part discusses the processes of preparing for, obtaining, and departing a superintendency. The socialization process that occurs as one is preparing for the superintendency is discussed and is followed by specific suggestions relative to obtaining a superintendency. The part concludes with a discussion of post-superintendency opportunities. A superintendency does not have to be the final step in one's career.

## PART FOUR (Health, Happiness, and the Superintendency)

If one is to provide committed and enthusiastic leadership for the duration of a professional career, it is necessary to achieve an integrated lifestyle with which one is comfortable. Therefore, this last part considers what is necessary for maintaining one's health, happiness, and yes, even sanity while serving as a superintendent. Life in the fishbowl and the unique problems encountered by single superintendents are explored. These are followed by ideas for controlling personal stress.

## CONCLUDING COMMENTS

The book concludes with a potpourri of comments on the superintendency. It does more than summarize. It talks about the synergism and excitement that await the superintendent of the nineties.

This book is written to blend theory and practice in a forward-looking mode. The information included has been obtained through research, interviews with hundreds of successful superintendents, and contributions from selected superintendents with special knowledge, experiences, and/or expertise.

There is no *how-to-do-it* list that will guarantee a successful tenure as a superintendent. If something can be *done by the book*, then by definition, it is not leadership. Each individual must take the information contained in this book, with other relevant information, and integrate and apply it to one's individual likes, strengths, and beliefs in order to be a leader. There is no substitute for the arduous process of thinking.

## REFERENCES

Long, G. H. (1988). Leadership and the pursuit of excellence. *Directors and boards, 12*, 21-25.

*What Works: Research about Teaching and Learning.* (1986). Washington, D.C.: U.S. Department of Education.

Shakeshaft, C. (1987). *Women in Educational Administration.* Beverly Hills: Sage Publicatons.

# PART ONE

# The Milieu of the Superintendent

An overall perspective and understanding of the setting in which the superintendent functions is a prerequisite to studying and understanding the superintendency. Thus, this subdivision on the milieu of the superintendent sets the stage for everything that follows.

# CHAPTER 1

# The Historical Perspective

A knowledge of history helps one understand the present. This adage is true of the superintendency. Contemporary attitudes towards and expectations of the superintendent are products of the history of the superintendency.

Interestingly, a detailed history of the superintendency is not available. Perhaps the reason for this is that the superintendency evolved as a product of growth in the public education arena. It was not a carefully orchestrated and planned addition to education. As such, a history of the superintendency must be pieced together from sketchy recordings dating back to the end of the eighteenth century. Wilson (1960) produced one of the few chronologies of the superintendency. His work will be used as a basis for much of the information in this chapter.

## THE STATE AND COUNTY SUPERINTENDENCIES

In the late eighteenth century the states became involved in education through the tenth amendment to the Constitution which says, "the powers not delegated to the United States by the Constitution, nor prohibited by it to the states, are reserved to the states respectively, or to the people." Since the word education is never mentioned in the Constitution, the states assumed responsibility for education when the citizens began expressing interest in mass education. The legislatures passed laws permitting public education and allocated small amounts of money to help local communities with their educational efforts.

When state funds began to be appropriated for education, the law-makers wanted some accounting of the funds. They often appointed volunteer committees to oversee these limited fiscal activities. These committees, formed at the beginning of the nineteenth century, were the forerunners of state boards of education.

As more communities availed themselves of state funds for education, work loads became burdensome for the volunteer committees. These committees then proceeded to identify a paid state officer to handle the accounting activities for them. Overseeing the state educational funds was but one part, and often a small part, of the state official's total responsibilities.

As the number of communities involved in state funding continued to grow, the oversight function became a full-time job. Thus, the first state superintendencies were established. New York is credited with appointing the first state superintendent in 1812. This practice was quickly adopted by the other states.

With but a few notable exceptions, such as Horace Mann in Massachusetts and Henry Barnard in Connecticut, state superintendents seldom exerted a strong educational influence. They primarily performed data collecting and oversight functions. These same functions are readily apparent in present day activities of state departments of education. For instance, establishing and enforcing minimum standards and equalizing educational opportunities through the distribution of state funds are still important functions of state departments of education.

As the population of this country continued to grow and expand westward, many hundreds of small local school systems sprang up. The task of visiting and inspecting these local systems became an impossibility for a single state school officer or committee. As a result, these responsibilities were gradually delegated to area committees. These area committees quickly became county committees. And, as happened at the state level, the volunteer county committees soon found the oversight activities too burdensome and proceeded to delegate them to a county official already on the payroll. As the responsibilities continued to grow, they required the attention of a full-time person. Thus, the county superintendency was born. More than a dozen states had adopted the county form of educational supervision before the Civil War. Today, the county superintendency is still very much in evidence in the educational governance structure of this country. In many states, the county office still serves as the intermediary between the local districts and the state department. In some states, the county office serves as the primary administrative unit and the county superintendent serves in the capacity of a local superintendent.

It is interesting to note that Thomas Jefferson had great foresight in comprehending the value of a county unit in the administration of public education. In his *Bill for the More General Diffusion of Knowledge*, which he introduced in the Virginia Assembly in 1779, he proposed that the citizens of each county in the state elect three aldermen to have general charge of the schools. The aldermen were to appoint one overseer for every ten school districts in the county. The duties of this appointee were to include appointing teachers, supervising teaching, examining pupils, and carrying out instructions of the College of William and Mary (Cremin and Butts, 1953).


## THE LOCAL SUPERINTENDENCY

The local superintendency was not the result of a sequential progression of the state and county superintendencies. Instead, it developed simultaneously with these positions. It evolved from local initiative and was not established by constitution or statutes as the state and county superintendencies were (Nolte, 1971).

Like its state and county counterparts, the local superintendency was preceded by a school committee which was appointed by the local councilmen or *selectmen*. Often the local minister served on the school committee as he usually was the most highly educated layman in the community. Unlike the state and county committees, these local committees were generally more reluctant to turn the supervising of the schools over to one individual. Perhaps this was because the responsibilities were generally limited to one facility, or perhaps it reflected the strong and much cherished independent spirit.

The first local superintendencies were established in the larger cities. Buffalo and Louisville are generally credited with establishing the first ones in 1837 (AASA, 1952). The practice slowly spread, and by 1870, more than thirty large cities had their own superintendents (p. 28).

Until the 1870s, local superintendents were employed by school boards without specific statutory authority to do so. They relied on the concept that the authority to operate schools also gave them the implied authority to hire an individual to administer them. The most famous case which legitimatized the authority of a local board to hire a superintendent was the Kalamazoo case in 1874 (Nolte, 1971). Although this meant that the local superintendency now had legal status, the duties and responsibilities of the position were left largely to the discretion of the local boards of education. To a large extent, this is still true today. As evidence, Garber (1956) performed a study of state statutes and concluded that the superintendent's legal status was nebulous at best. Also, Cunningham (1962) in a study of the decision making behavior of a large number of local school boards found that many administrative decisions, usually considered to be the province of the superintendent, were made instead by boards of education.

It was not uncommon at this time for the board members to maintain control of the business operation of the school, the part of the school operation with which they felt the most comfortable, and to delegate the instructional function to the superintendent. They also were very often involved in the personnel employment process.

It is interesting to note that the word *superintendent* has a Latin derivation. It comes from the Latin words *super*, meaning *over*, and *intendo*, meaning *direct*. This fits the description of the responsibilities of the early superintendents which were to oversee and direct the school operations. However, the derivation does not address the leadership and change functions. Perhaps history, and even the name itself, serve to make the leadership and change functions so difficult for today's superintendents.

## IMPORTANCE OF THE HISTORICAL PERSPECTIVE

Since 1950 when the first concerted efforts to study educational administration as an academic discipline came to the forefront, much research has been performed on school systems as organizations and on superintendents as educational leaders. As a result, we know more about school systems, leadership, boards of education, and superintendents than at any time in the past. However, it is interesting to observe that many of the factors which influenced the development of the superintendency still impact upon the superintendency today.

The superintendent as an employee of the board of education is still the law in most states. (In a few states, the superintendent is elected to office.) Unlike many professionals, the superintendent cannot operate autonomously. He/she depends on the board both for the establishment of policy and the approval of many administrative recommendations.

While progress has been made in defining the responsibilities of the superintendent, there is still much left to the discretion of the board. With some boards the distinction between policy formation and administration is blurred at best. This is particularly true in the financial and personnel areas. Seldom do boards get deeply involved in the mechanics of the instructional program. These contemporary relationships between superintendents and boards are remnants of past practices.

The early superintendents were expected to be reporters and managers but not leaders. To a large extent this is true today. A superintendent must possess a great deal of leadership acumen, knowledge about change processes, and patience if he/she is to truly function as the instructional leader of the school system. Citizens and parents tend not to view the superintendent as an educational authority whose ideas and views about education should be accepted as gospel. Instead, they develop their own beliefs relative to education in general and their local school system in specific. Furthermore, they often bring considerable pressure to bear on the local board and superintendent to have their views implemented.

In conclusion, an understanding of the historical development of the superintendency should offer some solace to beleaguered superintendents that things were not easy in the old days either. It also should lend a helpful perspective to the next chapter which discusses the contemporary setting of the superintendency.

## REFERENCES

American Association of School Administrators (1952). *The American School Superintendency*, *30th Yearbook*. Washington D.C.: The Association.

Cremin, L. A., and F. R. Butts (1953). *A History of American Education in American Culture*. New York: Holt, Rinehart & Winston.

Cunningham L. L. (1962). "Decision-making Behavior in School Boards," *American School Board Journal*, *144*:13-16.

Garber, L. O. (1956). "Superintendent's legal authority depends on his contract," *School Law*, 57:63-64.

Vlaanderen, R. B. (1971). "Statutory Status of the Public School Superintendent." In M. C. Nolte (Ed.), *Law and the School Superintendent* (pp. 5-50). Cincinnati: The W. H. Anderson Co.

Wilson, R. E. (1960). *The Modern School Superintendent*. New York: Harper & Brothers.

# CHAPTER 2

# The Contemporary Setting

## THE BIG PICTURE

Before discussing the contemporary milieu in which the superintendent functions, it is important to realize that each individual is unique with respect to the combination of personal beliefs and competencies which are brought to the position. These unique combinations are very influential in determining how each individual behaves in the superintendency setting and how others react to the superintendent; thus, no two individuals will react the same in the milieu of the superintendency. Furthermore, one's own behavior should change over time as one's personal beliefs are scrutinized and restructured via a self-assessment process which should be ongoing as one's competencies are honed and new ones acquired.

The competencies needed by a superintendent have grown rather rapidly in recent years, and existing ones have increased in importance. Table 2.1 presents a sample of the types of competencies required of a superintendent to function successfully in the contemporary educational milieu. In addition to these competencies, there are also a number of task areas in which the superintendent must be knowledgeable. Table 2.2 presents some of the more important task areas. As can be seen from these two tables, competencies and task areas are not mutually exclusive. For instance, strategic planning is both a competency and a task area.

Dr. Louis Daugherty provided the basic material for the "bureaucratic, open, and loosely coupled organization" portion of the chapter. Dr. Daugherty is a county superintendent in Ohio. Prior to assuming the county superintendency, he held superintendencies in two local school districts.

Ms. Rochelle Steininger provided the basic material for the "school system as a political system" portion of the chapter. Ms. Steininger is a doctoral student at Marquette University in Milwaukee, Wisconsin.

## TABLE 2.1. Superintendent Competencies

| | |
|---|---|
| Leadership | Change agent |
| A. Human | Computer literacy |
| B. Technical | Delegating |
| C. Conceptual | Enabling |
| Communicating | Empowering |
| Decision Making | Organizational dynamics |
| A. Problem identification | Group dynamics |
| B. Alternative identification | Resource management |
| C. Alternative selection | A. Human |
| D. Implementation | B. Material |
| E. Evaluation | C. Time |
| Strategic planning | Public speaking |
| Goal setting | Law |
| Motivating | Stress management |
| Risk taking | Time management |

## TABLE 2.2. Superintendent Task Areas

| | |
|---|---|
| Finance | Instruction |
| Budgeting | Policy development |
| Business management | Community relations |
| Personnel administration | State and federal relations |
| A. Pupil | Site management |
| B. Staff | Co-curricular activities |
| C. Evaluation | Strategic planning |
| D. Staff development | Transportation |
| E. Labor relations | Food management |
| Curriculum | |

The totality of the competencies needed by a superintendent and the number of task areas, some of which are quite complex, in which the superintendent must have a working knowledge is staggering. It is evident that the learning and inquiring processes are never over for the superintendent. There is always something new to be learned and skills which need to be refined.

The personal beliefs of the superintendent are used to help formulate a vision for the school system and serve as guideposts in determining how the superintendent's personal competencies will be applied in fulfilling superintendency obligations. Figure 2.1 depicts the application of personal beliefs and competencies to the educational organization or school system.

In addressing the contemporary milieu in which the superintendent functions, one is directed to the set of concentric circles in the middle of Figure 2.1. Two points should be noted. First, the largest concentric circle represents the world; and second, what is usually considered the educational organization is depicted only by the innermost concentric circle and the five overlapping circles within it. This graphically illustrates that the milieu of the superintendent is far greater than just the internal educational organization represented by the innermost concentric circle.

Primary responsibilities of the superintendent are to provide leadership in establishing a vision for the educational organization and then converting this vision into a set of goals and priorities for the organization. In order to do this, the superintendent must ascertain how students can be positive contributors to not only the nation but the world. Indeed, the technological age means that a world view must be developed. In the years ahead, products of the schools must be able to function on a global basis. The process of determining future global, as well as national, needs and resolving conflicts between the two is of great importance.

Worldwide events can have an impact on the daily operation of the schools. For instance, trade deficits, and in general, the relation of the United States' economy to the world economy have an impact on the level of educational funding. Thus, world events and trends have both macro and micro significance for the educational organization and are of considerable importance to the superintendent.

The national impact is similar to the world impact except that it is of greater magnitude and urgency. Changing national priorities, demographics, political climates, and outlooks on education have a signifi-

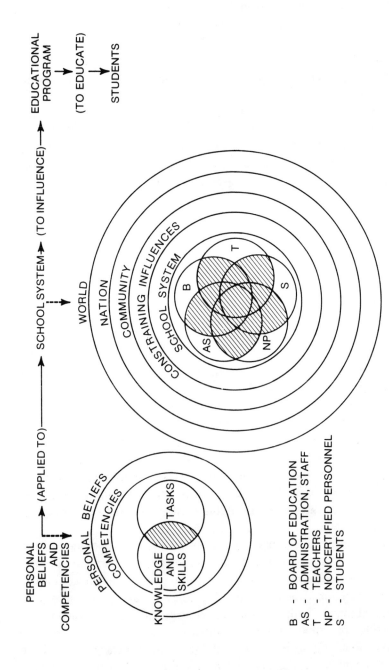

PERSONAL
BELIEFS
AND
COMPETENCIES

→ (APPLIED TO) →

SCHOOL SYSTEM →

(TO INFLUENCE) →

EDUCATIONAL
PROGRAM

(TO EDUCATE) →

STUDENTS

WORLD

NATION

COMMUNITY

CONSTRAINING INFLUENCES

SCHOOL SYSTEM

B

T

AS

NP

S

PERSONAL BELIEFS

COMPETENCIES

KNOWLEDGE
AND
SKILLS

TASKS

B  -  BOARD OF EDUCATION
AS  -  ADMINISTRATION, STAFF
T  -  TEACHERS
NP  -  NONCERTIFIED PERSONNEL
S  -  STUDENTS

*FIGURE 2.1. The Contemporary Milieu of the Superintendent.*

cant influence on the superintendent's formulation of a vision for the school system and the degree to which the vision is able to be fulfilled. Community mores, values, needs, and educational expectations are of utmost importance to the superintendent. As noted in Figure 2.1, the community is closer to the internal educational organization than the nation or world; and thus, it exerts the greatest immediate pressure and influence on the school organization. However, community concerns are often very parochial in nature, ranging over such matters as board member selection, coach selections, student transportation, facility utilization, etc. The superintendent must incorporate community needs and educational expectations with those of the nation and world in such a way that neither community mores or values nor the superintendent's are violated. Needless to say, this is no simple task.

The first concentric circle outside the school system represents *constraining forces*. These are forces brought to bear on the educational organization by people and organizational bodies outside the school organization that dictate, or attempt to dictate, how the organization will function. They serve as substitutes for leadership and include policies of the U.S. Office of Education, mandates and policies of state departments of education, federal and state legislation, judicial decisions at all levels, local referenda, and special interest groups. The school system and superintendent must operate within the confines of these parameters and at the same time not violate local community mores and values.

Finally, we have arrived at the innermost concentric circle, the *school system*. The actors within the system are represented by the five intersecting circles within the concentric circle. Theoretically, the board of education is elected by the community to set policies for and oversee the local educational program, and a superintendent is employed to operationalize and implement the policies. In reality, this is not the case. While the board does adopt policies, it is influenced in its adoptions by a number of significant others, with the superintendent being a very significant other. At times, such as in collective bargaining, the teachers and noncertified personnel can be significant others. At other times, the students fill this role.

The intersecting circles also represent overlapping efforts and responsibilities in the administration of the organization. The traditional hierarchical relationship is changing. As collaborative decision making becomes more sophisticated, as organizations have fewer layers of management, and as decision making becomes more decentralized, these circles will intersect to a greater and greater degree.

The superintendent must bring personal beliefs and competencies to bear on the educational milieu in an effort to influence the educational program. Everything that a superintendent does should work toward the development and implementation of an effective educational program which fulfills the vision, goals, and priorities of the local educational organization.

The superintendent is the only individual who must be deeply concerned about all areas of the educational milieu. Others will have their special concerns, interests, and responsibilities, but it is the superintendent who must juggle all of the balls in such a way that the local school system accomplishes its mission of providing a quality education for its students in an effective and efficient manner.

## THE SCHOOL ORGANIZATION

### The School System as a Bureaucratic, Open, and Loosely Coupled Organization

#### Schools as bureaucracies

Institutional environments use mechanisms such as rules, regulations, and inspections to produce their organizational effects. The survival of the organization is dependent upon conformity by most of the personnel within the organization to the institutional norms and procedures (Meyer and Scott, 1983). These mechanisms combine to form what is called the bureaucracy of the organization.

School systems commonly exhibit the bureaucratic characteristics of: a high degree of role specialization, centralization of authority in a vertical hierarchical structure, control achieved through formal policies, rules and role prescriptions, and functionally specialized units (school facilities). These attempts at formality are designed to promote maximum organizational efficiency and effectiveness. Examples of these bureaucratic characteristics are:

> *Division of Labor*: Elementary and secondary teachers; art, music and physical education specialists; and administrative, psychological, and counseling specialists are examples of *job* groupings designed to permit greater efficiency of oversight and function.
>
> *Rules and Procedures*: Job descriptions, administrative procedures, teacher and student handbooks, and board of education policies are

examples of formal rules and procedures created by school districts. *Hierarchy*: The superintendent, assistant superintendents, principals, department or grade level chairpersons, and teachers represents a traditional *chain of command* within school districts.

Detailed rules and procedures are also developed to help limit disruption by the external environment. For example, school boards adopt policies and procedures which limit public access to classrooms during the school day, parent communications with school personnel, and citizen participation at board meetings.

Another approach to limiting the impact of outside influences has been the creation of staff specialists who are not directly involved in the teaching-learning process. Personnel specialists, for example, are responsible for screening applicants to ensure that they possess the desired organizational characteristics and that non-desirable characteristics are either eliminated or at least minimized. In larger school districts, community relations staff persons attempt to serve as buffers between the system and its external environment. However, despite attempts to close the school organization off from these environmental influences, it is impossible and unwise to do so. In the broader perspective, the external environment provides the lifeblood of the school system and is the essence for its existence.

Meyer and Scott (1983) postulate that educational bureaucracies have emerged as personnel certifying agencies. They argue that, "they use standard types of curricular topics and teachers to provide standard types of graduates, who are then allocated to places in the economic and stratification system on the basis of their educational background" (p. 72).

Frymier (1987) indicates that in recent years, the states have assumed a greater governing role in education. The impetus for much of this change has been the national trend for greater accountability and reform in public education. The pressures for reform have ". . . forced superintendents to exercise tighter control at the central office level" (p. 19). He concludes that even though educators have been told to run schools like a business, they are being forced by these pressures to centralize and to do things only poor businesses do.

In conclusion, it is important to note that no formal organization can function without an operational bureaucracy in place. There must be guidelines for operations that are repetitive in nature. Consistency, stability, and formally established *communication channels* and *ways of doing things* are necessary to the efficient functioning of an organization. It is the role of the superintendent to see that the bureaucracy within his/her system is functioning properly. One must be alert to detect when the bureaucracy is too rigid and inflexible, inappropriately stifling creativity and innovation, delaying decision making, causing decisions to be made by the wrong people, functioning in inappropriate situations, and inappropriately influencing interaction and communication with external constituent groups. A properly functioning bureaucracy can save time for all members of the organization, and thus free them to spend more time on their primary functions and enable them to be more creative and innovative.

## Schools as open systems

Daft (1988) describes an open system as one which, ". . . must interact with the environment to survive; it both consumes resources and exports resources to the environment. It cannot seal itself off. It must continually change and adapt to the environment" (p. 11).

Open systems can be very complex. Internal efficiency sometimes is just a minor issue. "The organization has to find and obtain needed resources, interpret and act on environmental changes, dispose of outputs, and control and coordinate internal activities in the face of environmental disturbances and uncertainty" (p. 11). In this context, the organization should be viewed as a set of interacting elements (people and departments who depend on one another and must work together) that acquires inputs from the external environment, transforms them, and returns outputs back to the external environment. Thus, school systems that depend on their external environments for significant support and students and were in fact created by an external environment, are open systems. This necessary open relationship with the environment often creates uncertainty for the school district. The local community, state legislatures, governmental agencies, pressure groups, and employee unions are examples of external publics that can provide uncertainty.

It becomes a major responsibility of the superintendent to help the school organization cope with the uncertainty created by these external influences. This requires the superintendent to provide leadership that will help the district make the adaptations necessary to keep on course. Appropriate and timely responses to influential external environments result in a dynamic school organization which is constantly reacting, changing, and adapting, in a positive manner.

If one is not careful, responses to external demands can lead to unplanned substantive changes in articulated organizational goals. Thompson (1967) has suggested that organizational survival itself can become the central goal superseding formal and explicitly articulated goals. In order to cope with the pressures created by a changing environment, organizations may seek to satisfy basic primary needs, especially those that help ensure organizational survival. Simon (1957) has called this *satisficing* rather than seeking maximum efficiency in goal attainment. Although Simon's observation was made thirty years ago, there is still evidence of current-day satisficing by school districts.

### Schools as loosely coupled organizations

School districts have a penchant for planning. When this penchant is combined with the aforementioned bureaucratic and structural nature of school districts, it might be assumed that there exists a logical progression from mission statement, to goal development, to development of implementation strategies, to evaluation and revision of goals and strategies. If school districts were isolated from external influences, this probably would be a true assumption. However, due to the uncertainty brought on by external environmental dynamism, there often exists what Karl Wieck (1974) calls a loose coupling. In reality, action often precedes planning, and policies and practices are adapted later to reflect previous actions. This reversal is brought on by the system's need to respond to environmental contingencies, constraints, and changes. The threats and uncertainties presented by these changing environmental elements can cause school districts to react quickly and in ways that are not closely related to formally articulated goals and plans. The reactions often are more closely related to survival than to legitimate organizational needs.

It would be disruptive and counterproductive for the entire school organization to respond to each external pressure. One way in which a system avoids this general disruption is to create a new division or program within the organization to deal with a particular external influence. At times, there is a very loose coupling between the new division or program and the school district's goals. Two examples of such responses would be a drivers' education program and an alcohol or drug abuse program. It is important that these societal and individual needs be addressed, but they do not fit closely with what most would view as the primary missions of a school system. Perhaps these needs could be better and more efficiently addressed by other organizations.

It is the responsibility of the superintendent to recognize when a quick response is needed to an external demand. Should the school address the demand or should it be directed to a more appropriate organization? If the school is to address the demand, the superintendent must provide leadership to help ensure that the involvement of the system does not detract from, and hopefully supports, its primary missions.

It is worthy of note, that some programs which are initiated to address a specific, legitimate need often attain lives of their own and live on after the initial need has been satisfied. These programs, in short, become organizations within an organization and they have their own survival as a paramount concern as opposed to the missions of the school system. For this reason, it is wise, during periodic program evaluations, to review the program history to see if the original need for the program formation still exists and if the program is still fulfilling the need.

Internally, loose coupling causes problems with some very vital functions. Two of the problem areas, personnel evaluation and curriculum, are ones which are central to the recent school reform movement. In personnel evaluation, there is generally a weak formal inspection of teaching and student output (Meyer, 1983). These are delegated to the local school and are infrequent. Principals and teachers have little interaction regarding teachers' work. (This is particularly true of tenured teachers.) Limited day-to-day working relations exist among teachers at the same grade/subject levels. Student achievement is rarely used in teacher/school evaluations.

In the curriculum area there are ". . . few detailed standards of instructional content or procedure" (Wieck, p. 75). Students often are passed to the next grade with little regard for how much they have actually learned. Interdependence among instructional programs tends to be minimized.

Finally, it is important to note that there is a need for a school organization to be flexible and have the ability to respond to problems with dispatch when necessary. However, there also is a need to keep the school system headed in a direction leading to goal achievement. The system cannot function effectively if it is reacting at random to either external or internal pressures for change.

For a loosely coupled organization to stay on track, the individuals within the organization must know the mission and goals of the organization and be motivated to work toward their accomplishment. They must know the roles they play in the organization. Chapter 7 on "Transformational Leadership" addresses the leadership role of the superintendent in a properly functioning loosely coupled school organization.

## The School System as a Political System

### *Definitions of* Politics

One of the dictionary definitions of politics is "competition between competing interest groups or individuals for power and leadership" (Webster, 1981, p. 1,755). This definition fits the authors' view of the school system as a political system more closely than other definitions.

Tracy (1987) describes the school system as one "influenced by formal and informal power groups both within and external to the system" (p. 223) and adds that "an educational system can be assumed to have interest groups and conflicts similar to those found in cities, states, and other political entities" (p. 224). She adds as indicators of "the political nature of education": the existence of "differing goals and values represented by various interest groups"; conflict as "the norm rather than the exception"; and the fact that "external interest groups exert a strong influence over the policymaking process" (p. 224).

Cuban (1985) emphasizes that what is called "public relations" because of "occupational taboos" is actually politics: trying "to establish coalitions of groups and individuals who will support the mission of the schools and to minimize any damage done by critics" (p. 29). In the making of policy, "hammering out a consensus and the tugging and pushing that accompany this process are political activities" (p. 29).

Millman (1982) views politics in education, not as a negative, but simply the way things are. "Politics can be understood as the art and science of the possible. The main goal is achieved in pleasing the greatest number of people. . . . In effect, political decision making is a way of distributing the scarce resources among competing interests" (p. 26).

In a somewhat different vein, Bates (1987) discusses "cultural politics." He first defines "culture" from the perspective of the cultural studies movement as "a description of a particular way of life, (of a group or society) which expresses certain meanings and values, not only in art and learning but also in institutions and ordinary behavior" (p. 25). Thus, "cultural politics" is a "concept . . . that emphasize(s) the ideological nature of cultural constructions and the part they play "in the struggles between different groups" (p. 87). "Schools (school systems) can, therefore, be seen both as an ideological apparatus over which struggles for control will take place within the wide society and as sites within which struggles to maintain or challenge the existing hegemony are likely to take place" (p. 90).

Carnoy and Levin (1986) present another view as they describe the origins of conflict in the schools. They see the schools as an arena of conflict because they have the dual role of preparing workers and citizens. . . . That the educational system

> is charged with both these responsibilities creates within it the seeds of conflict and contradiction. The ensuing struggle between the advocates of two different principles for their objectives and operations tends to fashion schools that must necessarily meet the demands of both masters imperfectly (pp. 40-41).

## Politics in the History of Schools

Early rural schools were the "focus of people's lives outside the home" (Tyack, 1974, p. 15).

> They were the places where ministers met their flocks, politicians caucused with the faithful, families gathered for Christmas parties and hoedowns, the Grange held its baked bean suppers, . . . and neighbors gathered to hear spelling bees and declamations (Tyack, p. 16).

From their earliest days, schools were the places for gatherings but also for struggles of control. New schools were sometimes founded as the result of neighbor feuds (Tyack, 1974).

The population explosion, particularly in the cities, between 1820 and 1860 brought enormous organization problems to the task of education. Cities had neither the trained personnel nor the physical facilities to provide education for all children. Educational leaders looked to the emerging technology in the cities to help them "discover and implement" what they thought must be one best system of education. . . . The division of

> labor in the factory, the punctuality of the railroad, the chain of command and coordination in modern businesses. . . . They sought to replace confused and erratic means of control with careful allocation of powers and functions within hierarchical organizations; to establish networks of communication that would convey information and directives and would provide data for planning for the future; to substitute impersonal rules for informal. . . . In short, they tried to create a more bureaucratic system (Tyack, 1974, p. 29).

Thus, the burgeoning pluralistic society was confronted with new challenges and, as in earlier days, there were competing interests with solutions for those challenges.

The period from 1890 to 1940 was an era of centralization. Again, the struggle over schools as an ideological apparatus can be viewed as the central dynamic of this period, with "the members of a movement composed mostly of business and professional elites, including university people and the new school managers" (Tyack, p. 126) forming the group that came to dominate the schools during this period.

Spring (1984) provides an even closer look at the mechanisms by which this business and professional power elite came to control the school system during this same period in Cincinnati. Interestingly, Spring reports that it was the very notion of keeping politics out of school government which enabled this power elite to dominate Cincinnati's schools. Legislation was passed limiting school board size and providing for general, as opposed to district or ward, election. Thus, campaigning became a very expensive proposition. Since political parties were expressly excluded from this arena, only those with considerable financial backing could afford to campaign. In Cincinnati, the business and professional interests formed the powerful Citizens' School Committee which effectively controlled elections by controlling nominations and providing funds for campaigns. Challenges to this controlling elite arose in the 1960s, when "schooling had become one of the prime weapons in the war on poverty and a central concern not only of policy makers but also of the dispossessed, especially the people of color struggling for a greater share of power in the cities" (Tyack, p. 270).

Carnoy and Levin (1986) place these changes in emphasis within the context of the inherent conflict in the task of educating workers/ citizens. Since schools tend to be "conservative institutions," they will

> tend to preserve existing social relations. . . . In historical periods when social movements are weak and business ideology is strong, schools tend to strengthen their function of reproducing workers for capitalist workplace relations and the unequal division of labor. When social movements arise to challenge these relations, schools move in the other direction to equalize opportunity and expand human rights (p. 41).

From the economic perspective, Viteritti (1986) interprets the gains made in the 1950s and 1960s as the result of "client politics" that allowed the political system to respond to the needs of minorities, the poor, and the noninfluentials" (p. 243). But, as he notes, client politics works when the incentive for a small influential group to support policy outweighs the incentive for a broader political population to oppose it. In such cases, the client is the only active political constituency in the policy arena. It achieves victory by default because of the apathy of the larger community (p. 243).

The client of the urban schools, in spite of being composed of minority groups, is not small in numbers; hence, the costs are high, and even "particularly conspicuous in a period of decline" (Viteritti, p. 244). Thus, Viteritti presents an economic rationale, as opposed to class differences, as the basis for recent setbacks to programs for minorities.

Danis (1984) presents a microcosmic view of the political dynamics at work over recent periods with her case study of the school board of Santa Barbara, California, from 1930 through 1979. She concludes that before the major shifts in public attitudes could be translated into policies by the school board, school board membership had to be changed over several elections. Two periods of complete change during those years were highlighted by her study: 1931-1934, and 1973-1979. In the more recent period, three elections, in 1975, 1977, and 1979, resulted in a completely new school board and a new superintendent. Major changes in school organization and policies were effected during this period. By 1979, Danis notes, "The progressive era was over. Although the belief in individualization was never erased, in reality, the emphasis was on subject and/or functional proficiency, the ultimate goal being employment, not intellectual growth or social awareness" (pp. 141-142).

### Implications for Superintendents

Since history and current literature have clearly revealed the political nature of the educational system, and "keeping politics out of education" is no longer a credible excuse for denying the participation of diverse groups and interests in the process of this system, what insights might be offered for superintendents who must be immersed in this political milieu?

### Political Savvy

Danis, after a close look at the processes by which the will of the majority of the voting public manifested itself by replacing incumbent school board members, suggests that "The new superintendent, after an incumbent defeat, must not only understand the new mandate but must be capable of articulating and implementing policies and programs" (p. 142).

Millman (1982) advocates the understanding and expedient application of political behavior. He proposes some political maxims which may serve educators as well as they do politicians; for example, "Do not raise to the policy level those issues that can be handled satisfactorily at a lower procedural level" (p. 27).

## Superintendent Board Relationships

Causes of conflict between school boards and superintendents are misperceptions of roles and changes in membership that affect the balance of power according to Hayden (1986). He has some practical advice to offer, including clear definition of roles, a strong policy manual, and avoidance of any appearance of favoritism on the part of the superintendent. He urges superintendents to maintain a positive attitude, to be honest, and, if all else fails, to recognize that there are times when it is best to "terminate the relationship" (p. 19).

## An Ethical Framework for Politics in Education

Beyond the behavioral applications of political savvy is the question of the very purpose of the superintendency in the political system that is education. Bates (1987) notes that the definition of *success* will vary, depending upon the notion of culture to which one adheres. If *culture* means "high culture . . . one that claims to identify and celebrate the greatest achievements of the human mind," (p. 85) then

> administration can be judged as successful or unsuccessful according to how well it can reproduce that culture among those who have inherited it and produce that culture among those who have not or at least persuade those who lack such an inheritance that they are devoid of talent or worth (p. 91).

If, however, one adopts the cultural studies' definition of "culture" as the "whole way of life of a particular society," (Bates, p. 86), then

> educational administration can be judged successful when it helps articulate and develop the aspirations and maps of meaning that are the cultural inheritance of its members, thus, helping them to articulate and defend their interests in the wider social context (p. 91).

Bates' view of administration, he admits,

> is far from the "scientific," apolitical maxims of current administrative theory . . . for it involves not simply the formulation and implementation of reliable and neutral techniques of management but rather the active embracing of a political role involving analysis, judgment, and advocacy and the adoption of an active stance toward issues of social justice and democracy (p. 110).

In order to accomplish this in a particular school or system, Bates calls for an analysis of the actual culture, an analysis which may reveal that the culture of a given school or system is quite different from what it is believed to be.

Finally, Bates makes a strong case for an advocacy role for administrators.

> Advocacy, whether administrative or not, is inevitably suffused with values and ideology. The question then becomes: what overriding values are to inform the work of the school (or system)? Clearly, in any society that calls itself democratic, principles of respect for persons, social justice, and equity are fundamental. A case can also be made that the educational process, at its best, is also closely associated with such principles (p. 111).

## Summary

As noted at the outset of this section, politics is defined as competition between competing interest groups or individuals for power and leadership in government or other groups. This competition for power and leadership has been evident in school and system history from earliest times to the present.

The superintendent, the leader of the system, according to Bates cannot "keep politics out of education" but rather, must provide leadership in the political arena which is rooted in the "principles of respect for persons, social justice, and equity."

## CONCLUDING COMMENT

This chapter has attempted to *paint a picture* of the contemporary milieu in which the superintendent functions. The result is a chapter which is both lengthy in number of pages and diverse in content. This length and diversity reflect the extremely complex milieu with which the contemporary superintendent must cope in his/her efforts to provide educational leadership.

# REFERENCES

Bates, R. J. (1987). "Corporate Culture, Schooling, and Educational Administration," *Educational Administration Quarterly*, *23*(4), 79-115.

Carnoy, M., and H. M. Levin (1986). "Educational Reform and Class Conflict," *Journal of Education*, *168*(1), 35-46.

Cleveland, H. (1972). *The Future Executive*. New York: Harper & Row.

Cuban, L. (1985). "Conflict and Leadership in the Superintendency," *Phi Delta Kappan*, *67*, 28-30.

Daft, R. L. (1988). *Organizational Theory and Design*. New York: West Publishing Co.

Danis, R. (1984). "Policy Changes in Local Schools: The Dissatisfaction Theory of Democracy," *Urban Education*, *19*, 125-144.

Frymier, J. (1987, September). "Bureaucracy and the Neutering of Teachers," *Phi Delta Kappan*, pp. 9-16.

Hayden, J. G. (1986). "Crisis at the Helm: Superintendents and School Boards in Conflict," *The School Administrator*, *43*(10), 17-19.

Meyer, J. W., and R. W. Scott (1983). *Organizational Environments*. Beverly Hills, California: Sage Publications.

Millman, S. D. (1982). "Don't Get Mad Get Even!" *Community and Junior College Journal*, *52*(7), 26-28.

Simon, H. A. (1957). *Models of Man, Social, and Rational*. New York: The MacMillan Company.

Spring, J. (1984). "The Structure of Power in an Urban School System: A Study of Cincinnati School Politics," *Curriculum Inquiry*, *14*, 401-424.

Thompson, J. D. (1967). *Organizations in Action*. New York: McGraw-Hill.

Tracy, S. J. (1987). "The Positive Politics of Education," *Clearing House*, *60*, 223-225.

Tyack, D. B. (1974). *The One Best System: A History of American Urban Education*. Cambridge, MA: Harvard University Press.

Viteritti, J. P. (1986). "The Urban School District: Toward an Open System Approach to Leadership and Governance," *Urban Education*, *21*, 228-253.

*Webster's Third New International Dictionary*. (1981). Springfield, Mass.: Merriam Webster, Inc.

Wieck, K. E. (1974). "Educational Organizations as Loosely Coupled Systems," *Administrative Science Quarterly*, *21*(1), 1-18.

# CHAPTER 3

# The Future Scenario

Visualize for a moment the environment for which the schools will be preparing students to function in the year 2000. Science and technology will have reached a level of sophistication that is difficult to comprehend today. Cybernetic intelligence will be well along the path to implementation. Computers will be running many machines by responding to the verbal commands of the operators, and interactive electronic media will allow people to visualize events around the world and verbally interact with them. Medical capabilities beyond one's wildest dreams will be commonplace. Genetic engineering and bionic limbs will be in use. Many diseases will have been eradicated, and life expectancies will be longer. A revolution in the speed of electronic and transportation systems will have occurred.

Food supplies will be grown more extensively using hydroponic techniques. Sea farming will be commonplace. Scientific breakthroughs in fertilizers and harvesting techniques will enable even greater yields per acre.

The technological information society will have made quantum leaps. Businesses will be totally automated with electronic mail and filing systems, and paper letters and paper storage will be virtually unknown. Perhaps homes will be equipped to handle electronic mail. The only paper mail one might receive would be the junk mail that currently is so prevalent.

Futurists, such as John Naisbitt, feel strongly that human resources

Mr. David Kircher, an assistant superintendent in the Fairview Park City Schools, Fairview Park, Ohio, contributed information for this chapter. He has done extensive research relative to the future environment of organizations, particularly school organizations.

are the key to future productivity. He feels that the human element is far more important than structural and/or organizational considerations (Naisbitt, 1985). In other words, as we progress into the technological and information ages, human relations will become ever more important in determining success or failure in business.

If superintendents are to provide leadership for schools in this new age, there are five key areas which must receive introspection and analysis. These areas are visionary leadership and motivation, educational process and content, organizational restructuring and role redefinition, quality of work life, and effective use of technology. Each of these areas will be addressed in the following subsections.

## VISIONARY LEADERSHIP

Superintendents are often bogged down in the day-to-day realities of running a school district. Problems abound that need immediate attention. Such things as staff and parental concerns, financial problems, union demands, and legal problems combine to occupy vast amounts of a superintendent's time; however, if superintendents are to provide the leadership needed for the future, they must find time to transcend these immediate demands and become visionary leaders. They must develop in themselves and others a sense of mission regarding where their system should be going and an understanding of what is important in the school system.

One does not become a visionary leader by chance. It takes practice and effort to force one's own thinking processes, as well as those of others, to transcend conventional wisdom and thinking. It takes courage to think the unthinkable. In other words, one must make a start at being a visionary by entertaining creative and innovative thoughts.

The second stage in becoming a visionary leader is to help board, staff, students, and community refine the myriad of creative and innovative ideas into a mission statement for the school. The mission statement must then be converted to goals that are understandable and achievable.

The third stage is the motivational stage. The superintendent must motivate school personnel to accept and work toward the achievement of these goals. When this type of commitment takes hold in a school system, it permeates all thinking processes within the system.

In providing visionary leadership, the community cannot be overlooked. The public must be educated regarding the need for change in the schools. They need to be motivated to share the visions and excitement for the future with the school personnel.

## EDUCATIONAL PROCESS AND CONTENT

Superintendents must be involved in the rethinking of what the word *education* means. Does education take place only in the classroom? Or, with modern technologies, can students learn as well at home via computer or television? Toffler (1980) said that the notion that learning takes place only in the classroom is dated. Learning takes place under many modalities, of which the formal school setting is but one.

Thus, a new curriculum content and process will be required that must be based on the premise that students will have to be adaptable and flexible and will be involved in cooperative learning. There will be a new literacy.

What will the new literacy mean? Will workers still need to know how to read? Or, will they merely need to know how to interpret information given to them by talking machines and computers? Regardless of the answers to these questions, it is clear that the new curriculum must teach students to think and solve problems. It will no longer be possible to teach students facts alone because facts will be increasing at an exponential rate. Problem solving will be a key need for students. In their rapidly changing world, they will have to adapt and learn through a variety of modes. They will be on their own to learn new concepts. They will also need to be able to synthesize and analyze what is taking place around them in order to function effectively in a rapidly changing job market.

Adaptability and flexibility will be keys to success for students. It will not be uncommon for students to change jobs a number of times during their working lifetimes; therefore, they will have to be able to learn new skills at a rapid pace. This means that schools and businesses are going to have to work cooperatively. The private sector needs to have input into the curriculum. Schools, on the other hand, can help businesses by offering retraining services in new skill areas.

A final concept of the future school curriculum will be to have students working cooperatively in learning teams rather than individually and competitively. Roger Johnson (1988) captures the idea when he says that "none of us knows as much as all of us." His research has shown that people retain more when trained under cooperative environments; thus, he espouses team learning in the schools.

## ORGANIZATIONAL RESTRUCTURING AND ROLE REDEFINITION

Naisbitt (1985) and Toffler (1980) suggest that organizations must become less hierarchical and more responsive and innovative, meaning that there should be fewer levels of administration in school organizations. Many of the largest corporations in the world have already reorganized along these lines. Peters and Waterman (1982) found that the monstrous Toyota Motor Corporation operated with only five layers of management (as compared with Ford's seventeen). The eight-hundred-million-member Catholic Church also has five layers of management. Dana Corporation, which is a multibillion dollar corporation, has less than one hundred people at its corporate headquarters.

If schools are to follow these examples, hierarchical decision making will have to be reduced in favor of greater decision making at the building level. Collaborative networks will replace bureaucratic networks in significant decision-making processes. Superintendents will be spending more time in individual buildings stimulating those directly involved with the educational process.

As collaborative teams become the heart of the management process, organizational barriers will have to be removed so that all people can have direct access to each other on a daily basis. Free flowing networks will develop with people interacting with each other in the problem-finding and problem-solving processes.

Organizational restructuring will mean a redefining of many traditional roles within the system. Superintendents are going to have to empower the people closest to the problem to make the decisions, and then help and encourage them in the implementation process.

A major responsibility of superintendents will be adapting the school structure to support this new mode of operation and to help school personnel to be appropriately prepared to function effectively in this milieu. In doing this, superintendents will have to be good listeners. They will be constantly fine-tuning the organization as a result of formal and informal input from a variety of sources.

Finally, as decision making becomes more decentralized and participative, the traditional roles of school personnel will be redefined. The superintendent will be challenged to decentralize decision making without losing the overriding sense of mission that must continue to permeate the organization.

## QUALITY OF WORK LIFE

There are indications that all personnel within the school system are going to be placing greater emphasis on personal fulfillment and growth needs. The superintendent will assume a major responsibility for addressing the needs of these more fully actualized individuals. These needs include the physical and psychological environments and the acknowledgment of staff as professionals.

Attention will need to be given to the physical working environment to make it more stimulating, comfortable, and personal. Improving this aspect of work life will take some effort and money, but it should be reasonably easy to accomplish.

Addressing and improving the psychological work environment is a much more complex undertaking. In this area, the personal and professional needs of employees are not distinct entities. Items which enhance one's professional life also contribute to the well-being in one's personal life and vise versa. In addressing the psychological well-being of employees, it will be necessary to address personal needs such as providing child care facilities, flexible work schedules, permanent part-time and job-sharing positions, and individualized fringe benefit packages.

On a professional basis, greater involvement in curriculum development, pedagogical techniques, scheduling, teaching assignments, evaluation, and professional growth opportunities will need to be explored.

In summary, the best work will be performed in school systems that exhibit a sincere interest in addressing the personal and professional needs of their employees.

## EFFECTIVE USE OF TECHNOLOGY

The computer is the instrument that has ushered in the information age and has been responsible for many job changes. Computerization and robotics have made many jobs obsolete while also creating new jobs. However, the individuals whose jobs have become obsolete often do not have the skills to qualify for the new ones that have been created. Schools must address this problem by helping students understand that their learning will be lifelong if they are to remain employable.

Teachers and other school personnel need access to and knowledge of computers also. There are many functions that school employees still do manually that could be done more efficiently by computers. It is important for superintendents to develop an overall computerization plan for the district, provide the necessary hardware and software to implement the plan, and motivate and encourage employees to become active and enthusiastic participants in the plan.

Another technological advancement of the future is interactive television. This technology allows students to view television anywhere in the world and to verbally interact with the individuals at the source. For instance, world experts could be beamed into any classroom, students could enter into a dialogue with them, and small groups of students would then be able to take courses not normally offered. Possibilities for tutoring and adult education perhaps are even more far-reaching. In fact, the uses of this technology in the educational process are limited only by the imagination.

## SUMMARY

Formulating a vision of what the demands on schools will be at the turn of the century and how the schools can address these demands are imperatives for superintendents. Potential monetary problems in meeting the demands must not be used as an excuse not to do the necessary thinking and planning. Superintendents specifically and the educational community generally can't afford to be like Rip Van-Winkle and wake up some day to a different world in which the nation's school systems no longer play an integral part in the education of our country's youth.

## REFERENCES

Cetron, M. (1985). *Schools of the Future*. New York: McGraw-Hill.

Craver, C. (October 1983). "The Future of the American Labor Movement," *The Futurist*, p. 70.

Deutsch, R. (December 1985). "Tomorrow's Work Force," *The Futurist*, p. 8.

Johnson, R. (April 1988). Speech made at the annual conference of the Ohio Association of Supervision and Curriculum Development. Columbus, Ohio.

Kirst, M. (1984). *Who Controls our Schools*. New York: Freeman & Company.

Kotler, P. (September 1986). "Prosumer," *The Futurist*, p. 24.

Naisbitt, J. (1982). *Megatrends*. New York: Warner Books.

Naisbitt, J. (1985). *Re-inventing the Corporation*. New York: Warner Books.

Peters, T., & Waterman R. (1982). *In Search of Excellence*. New York: Warner Books.

Peters, T. (1987). *Thriving on Chaos*. California: Random House Audio-Books.

Raymond, H. (September 1986). "Management in the Third Wave," *The Futurist*, p. 15.

Sinetar, M. (March 1987). "The Actualized Worker," *The Futurist*, p. 21.

Toffler, A. (1974). *Learning for Tomorrow: The Role of the Future in Education*. New York: Random House.

Toffler, A. (1980). *The Third Wave*. New York: Bantam Books.

Venn, G. (1970). *Man, Education, and Manpower*. Washington D.C.: The American Association of School Administrators.

# PART TWO

# *The Superintendent as Leader*

The leadership part is the most extensive part in this book. This is as it should be, for leadership is the essence of the superintendency. The four subsections of this part are as follows:

A. The broader leadership perspective

B. Personal philosophy and leadership

C. Superintendent leadership competencies: personal

D. Superintendent leadership competencies: professional

# The Broader Leadership Perspective

# CHAPTER 4

# Historical Leadership Perspectives

It is necessary to have an historical perspective of leadership in order that the more specific leadership material presented in the three subsequent subsections can be viewed from an appropriate perspective. One must have some insights and answers to such questions as: What does the word *leadership* mean? How does one know it when one sees it? How does one know when one is providing it? This chapter addresses these critical questions.

## RECOGNIZING AND DEFINING LEADERSHIP

When Franklin D. Roosevelt died, Walter Lippman's syndicated column "Roosevelt Has Gone," April 14, 1945, stated that

> for the final test of a leader is that he leaves behind him in other men the conviction and the will to carry on....The genius of a good leader is to leave behind a situation which common sense, without the grace of genius, can deal with successfully (p. 4).

Lippman's definition of a leader was one who had an impact on others by giving them the conviction to continue. This conviction was not created through genius but through common sense. Just as Lippman sought to define FDR's leadership, the definition and concept of leadership have intrigued mankind for centuries.

Dr. Kathleen Ferrone provided the basic material for this chapter. Dr. Ferrone currently is the superintendent of the Strongsville Public Schools in Ohio. She has performed in-depth research on effective ways in which superintendents can provide leadership to their boards of education.

The Greeks, Romans, Egyptians, and Chinese have recorded observations regarding the act of leadership. Despite the varying cultures,
the following attributes of a leader emerged: justice, wisdom, coun-
sel, authority, valor, and judgment. During the Renaissance, in
Machiavelli's study of leadership entitled *The Prince*, he noted that
"there is nothing more difficult to take in hand, more perilous to conduct, or more uncertain in its success, than to take the lead in the
introduction of a new order of things" (p. 43).

James MacGregor Burns (1978) stated that "leadership is one of the
most observed and least understood phenomena on earth" (p. 2). In
his book, *Leadership*, Burns noted that although previous centuries
had been the seed bed of a richly illustrative compilation of literature
on leadership, the modern age has produced a fragmented approach
to the study and meaning of leadership as a concept. As an example,
there are over 350 definitions of leadership in the literature (Cunningham, 1985). Burns posits that there is no school of leadership, are
no standards of assessing leaders, and is no modern philosophical
basis from which one can adequately assess the empiricism and
theory of leadership. Consequently, modern man is left floundering in
indecision on the qualities separating leaders from rulers, power
wielders, and despots (Burns, 1978).

Warren Bennis, noted organizational theorist, developed a theory of
managerial strengths and tactics. In a bold step to put these theories
to the test, he accepted the presidency of the University of Cincinnati
during the early 1970s. This was the acid test for his leadership theories and for himself as a leader—a test made more challenging by the
turbulence on campuses during the late 1960s and early 1970s. Upon
leaving the presidency, he wrote a book entitled *The Unconscious
Conspiracy: Why Leaders Can't Lead*. In this book, Bennis reflects on
his experiences as president of the University of Cincinnati. At one
point he recalls that Clark Kerr, while president of Berkeley during
the heyday of student unrest, succinctly summed up the three most
important jobs of a president of a university: to provide sex for students, football for alumni, and parking places for faculty. Bennis
noted that at Cincinnati, sex is taken for granted, football was still a
priority, and parking was considerably worse. He then laments that
the times call for leadership but that leaders are not leading. Instead,
they are consulting, pleading, temporizing, martyrizing, trotting, putting out fires, and either avoiding the heat or taking the heat but
spending too much energy doing both.

Essentially, Burns and Bennis echo similar themes. Burns says that man cannot distinguish between leaders and power mongers while Bennis says that leaders themselves cannot distinguish between the concepts of leading and managing. Thus, the definition and recognition of leadership remains nebulous at best.

## HISTORICAL REVIEW OF LEADERSHIP THEORIES

### Great Man Theory

When Arthur Schlesinger, Jr. asked John F. Kennedy how he became a hero, Kennedy's response was, "It was involuntary. They sank my boat" (Bartlett, 1968). To paraphrase Shakespeare's great comic figure, Malvolio, in *Twelfth Night*, some are born to greatness, some achieve it, and some have greatness thrust upon them. Kennedy may have had greatness thrust upon him the moment his PT boat sank.

The great man theory of leadership embraces the notion that history is shaped by great men who have the capacity to lead the masses (Jennings, 1960). In 1841, Carlyle's *Essay on Man* reinforced the concept of a leader as a person endowed with unique qualities that capture the masses. Carlyle's hero would contribute no matter where found, because history is shaped by great men who are destined for leadership.

Would Chrysler corporation be what it is today if it were not for Lee Iacocca? Would the billion-dollar Disney Enterprises be just that, if it were not for the leadership and vision of Walt Disney? Without Moses, the Jews would not have left Egypt; without Churchill, England would have submitted. As England embraced Churchill in 1940, their collective political memory forgot that he had been in exile since 1934. Without Lenin, would there have been the Russian Revolution? If Lenin had been hanged and not exiled, and if the boxcar in which he traveled had not made it to the Russian border, the Bolshevik cause might have dissipated. Would American public education be what it is today if it were not for the likes of Thomas Jefferson, Horace Mann, and John Dewey?

The great man theory of leadership supports the idea that a superior leader emerges to lead a society no matter how intelligent, energized, and moral the society may be. A society cannot be led by the masses; therefore, a leader must always emerge.

Early leadership researchers reasoned that if the great man theory was valid then it should be possible to study these great men in an effort to discover the traits that made them great. Thus, in the 1920s and 1930s, researchers attempted to isolate the superior qualities of great men and in the process explain leadership in terms of personality and character traits (Bass, 1981). Many such personality and character trait lists were developed; however, no list was ever developed that guaranteed that if an individual possessed the listed characteristics he/she would be an effective leader. As a result, the trait approach to leadership fell into disfavor for a number of years. Currently, it is experiencing somewhat of a resurgence in that students of leadership are hypothesizing that perhaps there are certain traits that are necessary but not sufficient conditions for leadership. In other words, the possession of certain traits would not guarantee that one would be a leader, but it would be very difficult to be a leader if one did not possess these traits. As an example, it might be hypothesized that it would take a reasonably intelligent individual to be a leader of other intelligent individuals, such as in a school system. However, not all intelligent individuals will be effective educational leaders.

**Environmental Theory**

The environmental theory of leadership emanated from the great man theory. It posits that leaders emerge not necessarily because of their own inherent greatness, but because time, circumstance, and place surround them. The German philosopher, Hegel, noted that the leader fulfilled the needs of his own time; what the great man did was automatically right to do because he fulfilled what was needed. No man, however great, could change the course of history. The great man rose within the historical condition because the time, place, and circumstance were right.

Students of the United States Civil War could argue for the environmental theory of leadership by examining the person of Ulysses S. Grant. In 1848, Grant was a hero in the Mexican War, but by the 1850s, Grant had to resign his commission in the army rather than face being court-martialed for drunkenness. He returned to his farm near St. Louis only to find he could not farm the unyielding land, so he turned to selling real estate and failed at that. Near desperation, he beseeched his father for help. He was given a clerkship in a leather store in Galena, Illinois and proceeded to fail again. It became evident that soldiering was his forte; consequently, the outbreak of the Civil War was a fortuitous occurrence for him. He enlisted as a volunteer in the 21st regiment from Illinois, and by 1864, the once drunken failure had risen to Lt. General of the Army.

A half a century later and on another continent, one could ponder if Mahatma Gandhi could have been the perpetual thorn in the side of British India preaching nonviolence and civil disobedience if it had not been for the poverty, the religious and political factions, the discontent in India, and the decline of the British Raj. Could Martin Luther King have had the impact on the nation if it had not been for the emerging civil rights movement in the South? Returning attention to Vladimir Lenin, could he have returned to Russia in 1917 and begun a revolution if the time and circumstances were not there? Have the effective school and accountability movements had an impact on the type of individuals obtaining superintendencies?

The environmental theory of leadership embraced the ideas that the situation and the group were the significant factors in determining the type of leader who would emerge. Leadership was seen as residing not in the person, but in the occasion confronting the leader.

### Psychoanalytical Theory

Psychoanalytical leadership theory was based on the Freudian notion of the leader as the superego made real. Bass (1981) stated that the leader was seen as the father figure, a source of love or fear, and as an outgrowth of the followers' needs. As an example, Payne (1973) explored the adult Adolf Hitler from the perspective of childhood deprivations, the culture within Germany in the early years of the twentieth century, the political milieu of the time, and Hitler's relationships with authority figures. All of the above were combined in the horror that was post World War I Germany, a Germany that willingly accepted Hitler's philosophy.

M. F. DeVries (1977) studied the charismatic leader who, depending on his ability to control his own paranoia, serves the welfare of the group. The group, especially the dependent group, is devoted and unquestioning and succumbs to the charismatic leader in times of crisis. The charismatic leader is one who exudes confidence, dominance, and a sense of purpose and can articulate the needs and goals of the group and translate those goals into action. Charisma literally means *endowed with divine grace*. Qualities of the charismatic leader include, fatherliness, a high energy level, the capacity to inspire loyalty, and an optimism (Bass, 1981).

Were the days when a coach or band director went directly from coaching or directing duties into administration a reflection of the psychoanalytic theory of leadership in action? Many of these individuals tended to administer in a benevolent autocratic style. This style was usually accepted, and they were looked upon with favor. In essence, they were looked up to by the school staff and community.

## Interaction and Expectation Theory

Interaction and expectation theory implies that something is happening between two or more members of a group. As action/interaction occurs, group members participate in the action. In addition, this leadership concept embraces the notion of sentiment wherein a mutual liking takes place between group members. The clarification of group norms occurs when these positive bonds occur within the group.

Bass (1960) proposed that the quality of leadership is dependent upon the level of interaction in a given situation. Whether or not two individuals interact depends upon the size of the group, the geographical and social proximity within the group, the opportunity for contact, the level of intimacy and familiarity within the group, and the mutual attraction and self-esteem of the group. Leadership under this theory could be likened to the lever on a pinball machine that propels the steel ball along its course. Leadership is the act of initiating or structuring interaction.

R. J. House's (1971) path-goal theory is a prime example of the interaction and expectation theory of leadership. His theory is based on the concept that leaders clarify goals for their subordinates as well as the paths available to the subordinates to reach these goals. Leaders motivate the subordinates to perform, and in turn, the subordinates derive satisfaction from a job well done. The leader provides appropriate rewards for the positive performance of his/her subordinates.

## Ohio State Leadership Studies

In 1957, the Ohio State Leadership Studies staff with the development of a paradigm for the study of leadership (Bass,1960) ushered in a series of research studies and theories that viewed leaders' interactions with their groups and organizations in terms of some combination of task/relationship leadership style.

The instrument developed by the project staff was the Leader Behavior Description Questionnaire (LBDQ) and was designed to describe how leaders carried out their activities. Leadership was defined as the behavior of an individual when directing the activities of a group. Leader behavior was described in terms of two entities: initiating structure and consideration. Initiating structure defined the relationship between the leader and work group in terms of communication, procedures, and organizational patterns. Consideration referred to the affective relationship between the leader and members of the work group. The leader had a mixture of both initiating structure and consideration as part of his/her management style (Hersey and Blanchard, 1982).

### Fiedler's Leader Match Concept

Fiedler's theory is composed of two essential factors, the leadership style of the person in charge and the degree to which the leader can control or influence the situation. Leadership style is determined by the Least Preferred Co-Worker (LPC) instrument. The scores, which identify a dominate leadership style, obtained via this instrument lie on a continuum with a very high task orientation (low LPC) at one end and a very high relationship or people orientation (high LPC) at the other end. The leadership style identified by this instrument is viewed as an extension of one's own personality, thus, it is not possible to alter one's leadership style.

The three components that determine the degree of control or influence a leader has in a given situation are leader–member relations, task structure, and position power. Leader–member relations is self-explanatory. Task structure refers to the degree of specificity with which a task is to be performed. Position power refers to the degree to which the position of the leader gives him/her the authority to reward and punish subordinates. These three factors combine to determine whether situational control is low, moderate, or high.

Task-oriented leaders perform best in either a low-control or a high-control situation, relationship-oriented leaders perform best in a moderate-control situation. Therefore, if one's leadership style, as determined by the LPC instrument, is known, the situational control level at which this individual will function best as a leader can be determined. If there is not a good match between one's leadership style and the situational control level, then one must attempt to alter the situational control to a level that is compatible with one's leadership style. This is referred to as situational engineering (Fiedler and Chemers, 1984).

**Hersey and Blanchard**

In Hersey and Blanchard's (1988) theory, one's leadership style is determined via the Leadership Effectiveness and Adaptability Description (LEAD) instrument. Like Fiedler's theory, leadership style is a combination of task orientation and relationship orientation; however, unlike Fiedler's, leadership style is not confined to a continuum. Instead, leadership style can fall anywhere on a two-dimensional grid that places task orientation on one axis and relationship orientation on the other. Also, unlike Fiedler, Hersey and Blanchard believe that it is possible to alter one's leadership style because they view it in terms of behavior, which they believe can be controlled, instead of an extension of one's personality which cannot. They do believe, however, that one has a dominant preferred leadership style.

Situational analysis is determined by ascertaining the readiness level of an individual(s) in relation to a specific situation. Readiness level is determined by assessing the ability and willingness of an individual(s) to perform a task. The readiness level of an individual or group can range from very low to very high. A very low readiness level calls for a task-oriented leadership style, while a very high readiness level calls for a relationship-oriented style. The leader must start with a leadership style that is appropriate for the individual's or group's readiness level as he/she strives to raise it. It should be stressed that Hersey and Blanchard's definition of readiness is situation specific, thus everyone's readiness level changes with the situation.

## CONCLUDING COMMENTS

As theories of leadership have evolved during the twentieth century, the emphasis has swung from the study of the leader as an individual to an emphasis on the transactional leader who assesses, alters, and reacts to specific situations. At the present time, a new theory of leadership referred to as transformational leadership is emerging. It represents more of a holistic approach to leadership and holds great promise for the superintendency. In fact, the transformational leadership concept is viewed as important enough that an entire chapter is devoted to it in the next leadership subsection.

As one looks at the history of leadership, one discovers an overlapping of the various theories. Each theory adapts and builds upon another, and it is only by looking at the history of leadership that one is able to obtain an appreciation of its complexity and elusiveness. Influencing the actions and motivations of others is a very complex process that is far from being mastered. Herein lies the excitement in the study of leadership theory in general and the application of leadership theory via a superintendency in specific.

## REFERENCES

Argyris, C. (1976). *Increasing Leadership Effectiveness*. New York: Wiley.

Bartlett, J. (1968). *Bartlett's Familiar Quotations*. Boston: Little, Brown & Company.

Bass, B. M. (1960). *Leadership, Psychology and Organizational Behavior*. New York: Harper & Brothers.

Bass, B. M. (1981). *Stodgill's Handbook of Leadership*. New York: The Free Press.

Bennis, W. (1976). *The Unconscious Conspiracy: Why Leaders Can't Lead*. New York: AMACOM.

Burns, J. M. (1978). *Leadership*. New York: Harper & Row.

Cunningham, L. (1985). "Leaders and Leadership: 1985 and Beyond." *Phi Delta Kappan, 67*, 17-20.

DeVries, M. F. (1977). "Crisis Leadership and the Paranoid Potential: An Organizational Perspective." *Bulletin of the Menniger Clinic, 41*, 349-365.

Fiedler, R. E., and M. M. Chemers (1984). *Improving Leadership Effectiveness: The LEADER MATCH Concept*. New York: Wiley.

Hersey, P., and K. Blanchard (1988). *Management of Organizational Behavior: Utilizing Human Resources*. Englewood Cliffs, NJ: Prentice Hall.

House, R. J. (1971). "A Path Goal Theory of Leader Effectiveness." *Administrative Science Quarterly, 16*, 321-338.

Jennings, E. A. (1960). *An Anatomy of Leadership: Princes, Heroes, and Supermen*. New York: Harper.

Likert, R. (1967). *The Human Organization*. New York: McGraw-Hill.

Lippman, W. (1945, April 14). "Roosevelt has Gone." *The Cleveland Plain Dealer*. p. 4.

Machiavelli, N. (1940). *The Prince*. New York: E. P. Dutton and Co., Inc.

McGregor, D. (1960, 1966). *The Human Side of Enterprise*. New York: McGraw-Hill.

Payne, R. (1933). *The Life and Death of Adolf Hitler*. New York: Praeger Publishers.

Reddin, W. J. (1970). *Managerial Effectiveness*. New York: McGraw-Hill.

# CHAPTER 5

# The Uniqueness of the Superintendency

Viewing the chief executive officer's position from other positions within the organization is a difficult task. In most instances, individuals occupying other positions in the organization have never experienced the responsibilities and pressures of being a CEO. Therefore, others' perceptions of the CEO's position are formed by drawing conclusions from fragmented bits of information that have been gained in random fashion over a period of time. The net result is that the CEO position as perceived by the outside observer is usually dramatically different than the actual experience. A case in point is the manner in which building and central office administrators in a school system view the superintendency.

This chapter discusses the uniqueness of the superintendency as compared to other administrative positions within the school system. The principalship of a large high school comes closest to the superintendency because a principal in this situation is in charge of a self-contained operation of considerable complexity. However, as will be shown, even this position falls short of capturing the complete essence of the superintendency.

A dozen areas in which the superintendency is unique are presented in this chapter. While the sections are not entirely mutually exclusive, they do represent individual areas of uniqueness. The areas are not presented in any order of importance.

Mr. Daniel McCombs provided the basic material for this chapter. Mr. McCombs currently is superintendent of the Tallmadge City Schools, Tallmadge, Ohio. He has been a business manager, personnel director, and a high school principal.

## SCOPE

The most obvious uniqueness of the superintendency is the overall scope of the position. The necessity to look at the *big picture* is paramount. The superintendent has to be concerned not only with the activities at the various building levels, but also with the overall fiscal and political implications of these activities.

Boards of education and the community rightly hold the superintendent accountable for the efficient and effective operation of the district. In doing this, it is their expectation that the superintendent should know *everything* that is going on in the district. By contrast, the building principals and other administrators are held responsible only for those activities occurring within their domains. As another example, the principals and other administrators are primarily interested in garnering as many resources as possible to support their own operations. The superintendent, however, must always keep an eye on the big picture when making decisions relative to the allocation of scarce resources among these individuals. These decisions must be made in the best interests of the entire school system.

## PLANNING

A prime function of the superintendency is to provide planning and direction for the school system. More than any other employee, the superintendent must constantly be concerned with systemwide missions and goals and must be constantly working to motivate the other employees to accept and be committed to them. The superintendent is always concerned that the system is pulling together in a synergistic effort rather than operating as individual entities with missions and goals that may not support, and may even detract from, systemwide concerns. It is the superintendent's responsibility to be sure that every subdivision and every individual understand how their activities contribute to the big picture.

## RESIDENCY

The residence of the superintendent can become a significant issue with boards of education, as well as with the community. Many boards of education have a requirement that their superintendent live within the district as a condition of employment. This is in contrast to other administrators who usually are not required to reside within the district.

If one has aspirations to pursue a career as a superintendent, one should decide at the onset the stance that will be taken to a residency requirement. Because the longevity of superintendents averages from four to six years, it is likely that one will be facing this decision several times during one's career. In making this decision, a superintendent must weigh both the financial and emotional consequences. Financially, most boards will pay moving expenses, but they will not assume any of the costs associated with purchasing a new residence or selling an old one. Also, depending on the socioeconomic level of the district, residences of the caliber in which a superintendent will be expected to reside may be out of the economic range of the new superintendent. Emotionally, one must ascertain how the rest of the family will react to changing geographic locations and school systems.

## LONGEVITY

As alluded to in the preceding section, the average tenure of superintendents is reasonably short. By contrast, principals and other central office administrators enjoy a much higher degree of security and longevity. Declining enrollments or a shortage of finances that cause positions to be eliminated are exceptions to this generality. However, rarely are individuals in these positions as subjected to the whims of the board of education or the collective wrath of the community as the superintendent. When things go wrong in a district, it is usually the superintendent who pays the price.

## FOCUS

Building principals and central office personnel are usually more narrow in their focus than the superintendent. Often, they need only to be concerned with the welfare of their specific schools or programs. Actions taken by these individuals on behalf of their buildings or programs sometimes are taken at the expense of other buildings or programs. The superintendent must continually make economic and programmatic decisions based on the general welfare of the entire school system. The potential reactions from negatively affected building level and programmatic personnel can place a great deal of pressure and stress on the superintendent.


## COMMUNICATIONS

Central office personnel often spend the greater part of their day communicating within the organization. Principals have a greater responsibility to communicate with constituencies external to the organization, but with the exception of the high school principal, the greatest part of their day is usually spent on communications internal to the system and their respective facilities. The principal of a comprehensive high school comes closest to experiencing the complexity of internal and external communication demanded of the superintendent; however, any communication problem at any level will eventually find its way to the superintendent's office. Therefore, the superintendent must be concerned with the communication efforts of the individual administrators in addition to fostering and enhancing a districtwide image.

The superintendent must be extremely precise in his/her communications. Sloppy, incomplete, and/or misleading information furnished by the superintendent is taken more seriously and evokes a greater reaction than that coming from other sectors of the system, and such information can cause a great amount of chaos and damage to the organization.


## FISCAL EXPERTISE

In this age of expanding accountability and shrinking financial resources, most superintendents must become financial wizards in order to keep their districts financially solvent. School funding in most states is a very complex process, and woe to the superintendent who doesn't understand it. The business manager is the only other administrator in the system who has expertise in this area on a level to that required of the superintendent.

Many individuals enter the superintendency well versed in educational matters but very lacking in fiscal and business management skills. Exposure to business management concerns before entering the superintendency is a great asset. The experience gained from working daily with transportation problems, leaky roofs, unexpected utility increases, federal asbestos legislation, civil service laws, and obsolete physical plants will serve one well in the superintendency.

## LEVY CAMPAIGNS

In many states, boards of education have to go before the citizenry to obtain approval to levy taxes for current operating and/or capital outlay purposes. In these situations, it is the superintendent who is responsible for providing the leadership to determine such things as the type of levy, amount of money to be raised, and type of campaign to be run. Other administrators within the system probably will get involved in campaigning for the passage of the levy or bond issue; however, the overall coordination of the campaign and, in the final analysis, its success or failure will rest with the superintendent.

## LABOR RELATIONS

The superintendent and other administrators differ significantly in their roles in the area of labor relations. The other administrators, or their representatives, often serve on the negotiating team, and the principals are responsible for the day-to-day implementation of the negotiated contract. However, it is the superintendent who must help the board decide the system's priorities at the bargaining table. The superintendent must provide leadership on the following concerns: On which items can concessions be made and on which will the board hold fast? What issues are worth taking a strike over? What is the total cost of the proposed package?

Constant and complete communication with the board of education while negotiations are in progress is an extremely important responsibility which is solely the superintendent's. Others can help, but the superintendent must be in charge.

Determining the total cost to the school district of a proposed package is another important responsibility of the superintendent. One must be alert for hidden costs in a contract such as, professional leave, personal leave, class size changes, change in number or length of working days, and potential arbitration and factfinding costs. In some states, the superintendent must sign a legal document stating that monies will be available to adequately fund the negotiated contract.

## LOBBYING

Superintendents must be on top of pending and recently enacted state and federal legislation because it is important that they commit time and resources to influence pending educational legislation. This can mean working through and with professional groups such as the state association for school superintendents, the state school board association, the state department of education, etc., or it can mean making trips to the state capital when the legislature is in session to make personal contact with one's legislators and to testify at committee hearings. It also means getting to know one's legislators on a personal basis and keeping them informed about school related matters. On occasion, a superintendent will go to Washington to testify at a hearing. While testifying at the federal level is important and should be taken seriously, the greatest portion of a superintendent's lobbying efforts, however, will usually be spent at the state level.

Thoroughly understanding recently enacted legislation is extremely important. What does the legislation really mean for the schools? Often, innuendo and rash generalizations immediately follow the passage of significant school-related legislation. The superintendent must sort out the wheat from the chaff.

At times, state legislators pass educational mandates without supplying the necessary financial resources to implement them. The superintendent must be on top of this action immediately and inform the board of education and community of the potential impact of the legislation upon the school budget.

It is clear that no other administrative person in the system has the continuing lobbying responsibility and interest like the superintendent.

## DECISION MAKING

The school principals and the superintendent engage in a variety of decision-making exercises daily. However, the principals' decisions usually do not have as great an impact on the overall well-being of the school system as the superintendent's. For example, while the high school principal is anxious to make decisions that will enhance the morale within his/her building, the superintendent is concerned with the morale in each of the schools plus the mental outlook of the board members and community. Decision making in this milieu is extremely difficult.

## TIME ALLOCATION

All administrators within the system are extremely busy and have a great need to manage their time wisely. The superintendent is, however, the only one who has almost complete control over personal time allocation. The superintendent can determine which issues are worthy of personal attention and those that will be delegated. The superintendent should be able to do a better job of planning personal time allocation than the building administrators, because the superintendency is more isolated from the minute-to-minute operation of the school day than the principalship.

The superintendent also influences the way the other administrators within the system spend their time. This is done by direct request and by constantly communicating with them on what is important in the system. An important way in which the superintendent communicates to others what is important is the manner in which personal time is allocated and the manner in which the immediate assistants are encouraged to allocate their time. Allocation of time by the top echelon of administrators is not lost on the others.

The superintendent has a responsibility to allocate a greater portion of personal time to *thinking* than the other administrators. The superintendent is paid to be creative and innovative in idea generation and problem resolution. This will not happen if the superintendent's calendar is crammed nonstop with meetings that are interrupted only to handle the latest perceived crisis in the district.

## CONCLUDING COMMENTS

Twelve areas have been put forth which, when taken together, make the superintendency a very unique position within the school system. The breadth and complexity of the responsibilities that go with the superintendency, along with the fact that the superintendent has the ultimate responsibility for the performance of all aspects of the system, make the superintendency an awesome, and at times, an overwhelming position. Some individuals thrive in this milieu. Others become hesitant and timid at the thought of making decisions that have a significant impact on many lives, both students and staff, and that will constantly be communicated broadly and receive continuing and close scrutiny. The fact that one often has to stand alone can be frightening; there are no other superintendents in the school system.

One can prepare thoroughly and conscientiously for the superintendency, but it is difficult to predict how one will function in the top chair until one occupies it. Many terrific assistant coaches never quite make it as the head coach. Any experience one can gain prior to obtaining a superintendency in assuming decision-making responsibilities that are public and have an impact on individuals with diverse interests will be beneficial.

On the positive side, some individuals thrive in this milieu. The challenge, excitement, responsibility, and opportunity to positively affect the lives of many individuals keep the adrenaline flowing and put a bounce in one's step. The job becomes more important than the individual, and the mission assumes a status that is greater and more important than personal job security.

# Personal Philosophy and Leadership

# CHAPTER 6

# A Philosophical Discussion

A very influential member of your school board has just called and given you a strong recommendation relative to the employment of a personal friend for a teaching position. How are you going to handle this recommendation which, as presented, is tantamount to a directive? Your personal philosophy as it is applied to the administrative process will be used as a guideline in weighing the pros and cons of the various alternatives you will consider en route to making a decision on this matter.

The preceding paragraph depicts a specific dilemma for the superintendent. A more general example could involve making decisions on how to implement the effective schools research. For instance, in the name of increasing *school effectiveness*, elaborate goal-setting and measurement techniques have been and are being developed along with a host of *technical tools* to help individuals operate more effectively within the organization. Today, more than at any time in history, more is known about how organizations (specifically school organizations) and individuals react. However, an often overlooked fact is that individuals and organizations can use this knowledge to help achieve any goals, good or bad. Thus, organizational effectiveness is determined by deciding which goals are worthy of achieving regardless of the leadership techniques used. But how can *good* educational goals be distinguished from *bad* ones? One's personal philosophy is critical in deciding which goals will be established to achieve an *effective school program*.

This chapter was adopted from an article written by William Konnert and Orin Graff entitled, "The Sine Qua Non of Organizational Effectiveness" that appeared in the Fall, 1976 edition of *The Educational Administration Quarterly*.

The influence of one's personal philosophy in the decision-making process is inescapable. Thus, a discussion of one's personal philosophy is not a useless academic exercise; rather, it represents an attempt to address the most important factor in the decision-making process. In fact, consistent decision making is dependent upon adherence by leaders to a personal philosophy or set of values that keeps them *honest* in their behavior. What follows is a discussion of the components of a personal philosophy, and the role one's personal philosophy plays in educational philosophy and professional decision making.

## THE SINE QUA NON OF ORGANIZATIONAL EFFECTIVENESS

Every individual's personal preferences, habits, and values, in one way or another, come into play with every decision made. Preferences and habits, often unconsciously held, are for the most part environmentally acquired and in part, custom based on experience.

Values are of a different order because they are an individual's more conscious recreations of habits and preferences, deliberately used to direct personal experience and/or to achieve personal goals. Thus, values are the stuff of which a personal philosophy is made. Yet, there is a further step in the achievement of a personal philosophy: the various values held by an individual must be compatible, else an analysis of overt action is apt to reveal an amazing jumble of inconsistencies. The achievement of compatibility among values is a responsibility that only the individual can assume. Obviously, complete compatibility can never be completely achieved because intelligent action requires, as an important aspect of life, the evaluation and regeneration of one's values as new, productive experiences, both personal and vicarious, are lived.

An individual's values are not separated from one's acquired preferences and habits, but rather are the results of choices resulting from appraisal of personal behaviors. A personal philosophy is achieved by continuously seeking compatibility among the values to which one becomes committed.

One other important aspect of a personal philosophy needs to be noted. Compatibility among values is hardly possible without arranging them in an orderly fashion from general to specific, major to minor, and concern for others to concern for self. Thus, one's philosophy is lifted from the status of a hodgepodge of specific values to an organized and understandable unity of values. A central core of values provides a person with a personal evaluative base for both present and projected action. Without such a core of values in operation, a person cannot be judged to have a philosophy.

Perhaps the most important element in the core of a personal philosophy should be the all-pervading desire to place human welfare above all other concerns. Essentially, this tenet means that whatever decisions are made and implemented, projected outcomes must be in the interests of those most likely to be affected, including of course, the individual or individuals immediately involved.

An overriding concern for the welfare of others should then be the chief factor in integrating an individual's values into a consistent, comprehensive, and workable whole, thus achieving a personal philosophy. The concern for the welfare of others constitutes a basic and integrating factor in any personal philosophy. The neglect for the welfare of others in the creation of a philosophy is an exercise in futility for a superintendent.

It is legitimate to speak of an organizational philosophy; however, the primacy of the interaction of individual personal philosophies in establishing an organizational philosophy is self-evident. The philosophy of an organization is a constellation of consistent values, the components of which are derived from the values of those who are responsible for the management, control, and direction-setting functions within the organization. Thus it is impossible to promote into action, values that are not held and commonly supported by individuals within the organization. Further, these values constitute a strong motivating force for productivity if commonly held by a majority of the work force within the organization.

A philosophical base is the sine qua non to organizational effectiveness and sound decision making. The real basis for decisions, and ultimately organizational effectiveness, goes far beyond the use of leadership techniques. It is through only a well-conceptualized philosophical base that worthy goals can be established and appropriate leadership techniques selected to facilitate their achievement.

## DEVELOPMENT OF THE SINE QUA NON

Organizational leaders have the difficult task of avoiding the *how-to-do-it* syndrome. A checklist is easy to follow compared to the hard philosophical thought process. If practical advice and *common sense* are the guides to practice, then all aspects of theory are ignored as nonfunctional. Under such conditions, the value base of administrative leadership is ignored; either the persons involved falsely assume that whatever is done will generally affect others positively or they confuse immediate self-satisfaction with the common welfare.

The formulation of a personal philosophy is a tough and time-consuming task for a mature person who, for the first time, decides to sort out personal values and re-order life activities accordingly. No one really enjoys viewing in retrospect a hodgepodge of inconsistent behavior or dealing with the problems of discarding firmly established attitudes and modes of behavior. One may know what one ought to do, but there is still a strong urge to continue past modes of behavior. Such attitudes and feelings can be controlled only if one pushes, and continues pushing, oneself into acting as one knows one ought. It is only through this kind of thinking and testing in everyday life situations that a person achieves a personal philosophy that is consistent, comprehensive, and workable.

By its very nature, a personal philosophy is a dynamic, directing, and controlling human behavior, and as such, has the capacity for growth and change. A philosophy in action should find the possessor relatively, but never entirely, satisfied with the results. There is always a definite feel that the results could be improved. This constant personal demand for higher congruity between ideals and practice is the kind of challenge needed to give lifelong attention to the improvement of one's personal philosophy—to maintain and enhance its dynamic state.

It is even more difficult for a group of persons to develop and maintain a philosophy for their organization than for each to develop and maintain a personal philosophy. However, establishing an adequate philosophic value base for an organization with a membership lacking in adequate personal philosophies is futile.

## APPLICATION OF PERSONAL PHILOSOPHY TO DECISION MAKING

To illustrate the application of one's personal philosophy to decision making, the thinking process involved in reaching a decision to the situation put forth in the opening paragraph of this chapter will be explored.

In addressing this situation, let us assume that your personal philosophy places an extremely high priority on the welfare of others. When applied to your school system, this stance means that you have a paramount concern for the education of the students. If this is the case, then your decision regarding this particular sample situation seems rather clear-cut. You hire the best qualified teacher for the position, without regard to personal friendships. However, upon closer inspection, this decision may not be so cut-and-dried. For instance, suppose you strongly believe that a much greater emphasis on professional inservice within your system is the best way to enhance the quality of education within your district. To this end, you have been working with the board in an attempt to convince the members to add one week to the contract of each teacher. This additional week will be used exclusively for professional enhancement activities without students present. This move will mean the addition of another fifty thousand in salaries to an already tight budget. In addition, you will need another ten thousand dollars to conduct a quality program during this additional week. Presently, the community sees no need to spend more money on inservice activities. In short, if the board is to adopt and fund your plan, it will mean that each member will be making a high-personal-risk decision. If your plan is to have any chance of receiving board approval, you must have the support of the influential member who just made the call to you.

In analyzing the above scenario, you might decide that in the big picture, the students in your entire system will be better served by the inservice program. This logic could be particularly valid if the difference between the board member's friend and the other individual you would prefer to employ is not great. Thus, it might be best to employ the board member's friend in order to enhance the probability of board acceptance of the inservice program. You tend to be leaning in this direction. However, it also occurs to you that if you hire the board member's friend, you might be setting a precedent for board member involvement in employment that could have long-term disastrous effects on the system. If this is the case, the negative precedent set by the employment of this teacher outweighs even the proposed inservice program. So, now you are beginning to think that the best plan of action would be to not employ the board member's friend. The decision is not easy. However, you are not wavering on your intention of making the decision in light of what you believe is in the best interests of the students in your system. The pros and cons of the various alternatives must be weighed against this dominant guideline. After you have made the decision, you will decide how to deal with the board member and the members of your staff.

For now, let's approach the above scenario from a different perspective. Suppose you know a superintendent who is very self-serving. This individual values career advancement above all else. You suspect that this individual would find this decision, which is driving you up the wall, relatively easy to make. He would strike a deal with the board member for a strong recommendation at some future date, or for something else of a similarly self-serving nature, in return for the employment of the board member's friend. For just a moment, you are a bit envious of your cohort; however, you quickly realize that this way of thinking is not you. A quick mental recap of what you expect to accomplish in the superintendency puts you in a better frame of mind and both excited and confident about wrestling with the problem in light of your own values.

In summary, the above discussion was intended to illustrate that your value base guides you in making the tough decisions. It doesn't make the decisions for you. For as we have seen, differing sets of circumstances can lead to differing decisions. Rather, it provides the benchmark against which various alternatives are weighed. At times, you will even make the same decision as someone operating from a substantially different value base. As this is the case, one can mask one's real values for a while, if one is so inclined. However, sooner or later the real you and your real value system will emerge for all to see.

## CONCLUDING COMMENTS

The thesis of this discussion is that the effectiveness of an organization depends on the values of the individuals involved; thus, the personal philosophies from which the individuals operate are the sine qua non for organizational effectiveness. More than any other factor, they determine the organizational philosophy and goals that will be established and to which people within the organization will be committed. They also condition the leadership techniques to be applied in reaching those goals.

In addition to demonstrating a need for the importance of a good philosophical base, this discussion has further proposed a belief that such a base should be grounded in an overriding concern for the welfare of others in achieving unity among the complex variables at play within society and within the school organization.

Judgments and decisions that are based on a well-thought-out philosophical base applied to relevant data is the only route to achieving trust and confidence among the membership of an organization, and is essential for the contemporary leader seeking to cope effectively with a myriad of complex situations. Without it, a leader will find it extremely difficult to place a proper perspective on the many situations confronted daily.

This discussion has important implications for personnel selection. Often an individual's philosophical base is not given serious consideration in the selection process. Such a process is inadequate if the aim is to select those who will be of the greatest benefit to the organization. The nature and consistency of the values of a selectee must rank high among selection criteria; in fact, they must be given top priority.

In conclusion, the philosophical base and corresponding values of individuals concerned with organizational leadership will be key ingredients to organizational effectiveness. The skill with which a leader can apply one's technical knowledge and leadership techniques to the organization and not violate one's own philosophical base will, in the long run, determine the degree of personal and organizational effectiveness achieved. A sound and internally consistent philosophy is the sine qua non upon which leadership is based and consequently, the ethical base for organizational effectiveness.

# CHAPTER 7

# Transformational Leadership

In order for a superintendent to bring about positive change within a school system, a mission statement with accompanying goals and objectives must be developed that is consistent with one's personal philosophy. Secondly, the development of a system culture and value system that support these goals and objectives and to which those associated with the system are committed must be created. In order to provide effective leadership in bringing all of this to fruition, the superintendent must go beyond transactional leadership to become a transformational leader.

This chapter describes transformational leadership and delineates the differences between a transactional leader and a transformational leader. It describes a different form of leadership thinking for the superintendent.

## WHAT IS TRANSFORMATIONAL LEADERSHIP?

James MacGregor Burns (1978) suggested that only a portion of leadership is due to an exchange or transaction between the leader and followers. In transactional leadership, the leaders and followers approach each other with the expectation that an exchange will occur.

Dr. Frances Murray provided the basic material for the "What Is Transformational Leadership" portion of this chapter. Dr. Murray currently is a vice president at Notre Dame College in Ohio. Prior to obtaining this position, she served as a high school principal for many years. She recently completed a comprehensive study of transformational leadership within educational organizations.

Mr. Richard Clapp provided the basic material for the "Transformational Leadership and Organizational Culture" portion of this chapter. Mr. Clapp currently is superintendent of the Woodridge Local Schools in Ohio. He has performed extensive research on school cultures.

In going beyond this approach, the transformational leader "looks for potential motives in followers, seeks to satisfy higher needs, and engages the full person of the follower. The result of transformational leadership is a relationship of mutual stimulation and elevation . . ." (p. 4).

Bennis (1984) detailed the following competencies common to transformational leaders:

1. *Management of attention*: a compelling vision which brings others to a place they have not been before; a clear sense of outcome, goal, and direction.

2. *Management of meaning*: communicating the vision; making dreams apparent to others and aligning people with these dreams.

3. *Management of trust, constancy, and focus*.

4. *Management of self*: knowing one's skills and deploying them effectively (p. 17).

Tichy and Ulrich (1984) and Tichy and Devanna (1986) characterized transformational leaders as (a) identifying themselves as change agents; (b) being prudent risk-takers; (c) believing in people; (d) being value-driven; (e) being lifelong learners; (f) being able to deal with complexity, uncertainty, and ambiguity; and (g) being visionaries. The following quotation summarizes their findings:

> What is required of this kind of leader is an ability to help the organization develop a vision of what it can be, to mobilize the organization, to accept and work toward achieving the new vision, and to institutionalize the changes that must last over time (Tichy and Ulrich, 1984, p. 59).

In comparing transactional and transformational leadership, Bass (1985) described the transactional leader as one who recognizes what subordinates want to derive from their work and provides appropriate rewards for expected performance, i.e., responds to subordinates' immediate self-interests. In addition, his research yielded the following two factors associated with transactional leadership:

1. *Contingent reward*: the leader is seen as frequently telling subordinates what must be done to achieve a desired reward for their efforts.

2. *Management-by-exception*: the leader avoids giving directions if old ways are working; leader intervenes only if standards are not being met.

Bass (1985) describes transformational leadership as motivating subordinates to do more than they ever expected to do by raising their level of awareness and consciousness about the importance and value of reaching designated outcomes, encouraging subordinates to transcend their own self-interests for the sake of the organization, and altering subordinates' needs on Maslow's hierarchy or expanding their portfolio of needs and wants. He has identified three transformational leadership factors, which are as follows:

1. *Charisma*: the leader instills pride, faith, respect; has a gift for seeing what is really important; has a sense of mission (vision) effectively articulated.

It is important to note that inspirational leadership is a subfactor of charismatic leadership which ". . . appeals to faith rather than reason, and to the emotions rather than the intellect" (Bass, 1985, p.65). The principal components of inspirational leadership include an action orientation in contrast to a focus on constraints, prerogatives, precedents, and formalisms; confidence building based on reality and truth; and belief in greater causes. "People who come to believe they are working for the best company with the best products are ready to exert extra effort" (Bass, 1985, p.67).

2. *Individual consideration*: the leader delegates projects to stimulate and create learning experiences; treats each person with respect and as an individual.

From a practical perspective, individual consideration takes many forms. It can be accomplished by such means as expressing appreciation for a job well done, constructive notice of weaknesses, delegation of special projects to utilize special talents and promote subordinate self-confidence, reduction of role ambiguity, face-to-face contact with subordinates, being a good listener, and mentoring.

3. *Intellectual stimulation*: the leader provides ideas which result in a rethinking of old ways; leader enables followers to look at problems from many angles and to seek creative solutions.

With respect to intellectual stimulation, Bass cautioned that merely being a person of ideas is not, in itself, sufficient. One must also engage followers in analysis, formulation, implementation, interpretation, and evaluation (Wortman, 1982).

Transformational leaders are less willing to be satisfied with partial answers and to accept the status quo, and they are more likely to seek new ways and take maximum advantage of opportunities despite higher risks. They are proactive, creative, novel, and innovative. By contrast, transactional leaders are concerned with how best to keep the organization running. They are ever mindful of organizational constraints, and they focus on conservative stances and seek to use old symbols in old ways.

In summary, "the transactional leader works within the organizational culture as it exists; the transformational leader changes the organizational culture" (Bass, 1985, p.24). Transactional leadership yields expected performance while transformational leadership yields performance beyond expectations (Bass, 1985).

## TRANSFORMATIONAL LEADERSHIP AND THE ORGANIZATIONAL CULTURE

Before a transformational leader can change an organization's culture, one must first understand what an organizational culture is and by what means it can be changed. The next section discusses the organizational culture concept. This is followed by a section identifying ways in which an organizational culture can be changed.

### What is an Organizational Culture?

Schein (1987) defines *culture* as:

a pattern of basic assumptions — invented, discovered, or developed by a given group as it learns to cope with its problems of external adaptation and internal integration — that has worked well enough to be considered valid and, therefore, to be taught to new members as the correct way to perceive, think, and feel in relation to those problems (p. 9).

In short, an organization's culture determines *how things are done around here*.

Johnston (1987) indicates that "at the very foundation of a culture are its values — basic beliefs that control the choices we make" (p. 80). Every organization has these values. If they are true organizational values, they are believed and subscribed to by most members of the organization. They are the bedrock of the organization, and they indicate what the organization stands for and determine how it conducts its affairs. They are institutionalized and guide and control the behavior of the individuals within the organization.

Outstanding organizations have a core set of values that are extremely important and must be observed. Organizational members display a dedication to these values that has been referred to as rigid, nonnegotiable, inflexible, and fanatical. They are willing to confront anyone within the organization who might be so brazen as to disregard them. Enforcement is placed above personal popularity (DuFour and Eaker, 1987). The unwillingness by organizational members to accept excuses for a lack of adherence to core values makes it clear that they are important and should be incorporated into daily practices (Johnston, 1987). In further support of a core set of values, Peters and Waterman (1982) state:

> . . . suppose that we were asked for one all-purpose bit of advice for management, one truth that we were able to distill from the excellent companies research. We might be tempted to reply, 'Figure out your value system. Decide what your company stands for' (p. 279).

Thus, it is essential that schools develop a core set of values that are shared by teachers, administrators, board members, parents, and citizens (Deal, 1985). It is the shared values that keep the various subgroups within the school organization headed in the same general direction, and is also a set of core values that will make empowerment work. For, as decision making is decentralized, it is imperative that the decision makers adhere to a common set of values. Otherwise, a series of subgroups with different goals, heading in different directions, and at times working at odds with each other, will be the result.

A number of examples can be put forth where an organization's values have a profound impact on its operations. For instance, in a school organization, values will determine such things as whether academics or athletics are given higher priority, whether women and minorities can obtain formal leadership positions, the importance of achievement test scores, the emphasis placed on a warm and caring environment, and the things to which employees are willing to devote extra time and effort.

## Shaping Organizational Values

Organizational leaders must give high priority to the shaping and dissemination of appropriate organizational values. If these values are to survive, they must be nourished and celebrated (Deal and Kennedy, 1982). Deal (1985) identifies six ways in which organizational values may be shaped.

## Document the school's history

A school system's history should be explored and documented. Important events and people should be chronicled for all to read. Shared values evolve from experience and have historical analogies. "Values detached from history rarely have meaning" (p. 616).

### Anoint and celebrate heroes and heroines

These need to be individuals who embody and represent the school system's core values. They need to be recognized not only for themselves but also for the important value(s) they represent. Thus, the recognition can be situation specific.

Recognition can be accomplished via storytelling of the type that abounds at reunions. Ways need to be devised to share these tales of the past with each new generation of students.

Recognition also can be done through materialistic symbols. The New York Yankees have celebrated their immortals with statues in center field. There is a statue of Stan Musial outside of Busch Stadium in St. Louis. Some schools have established "Walls of Fame" where they honor their distinguished graduates. Every high school has a trophy case, and most have an entire hallway devoted to athletic feats of the past.

Johnston (1987) believes that the impact of heroes on the school is profound in that it:

1. shows that success is attainable and human;
2. provides role models for other group members;
3. creates a school image for the outside world;
4. sets standards of performance; and,
5. motivates people to perform. (p. 84)

### Rituals

Rituals determine much of the day-to-day behavior in any organization. The school's rituals should be reviewed periodically to be sure they are reinforcing the appropriate values. They should also be reviewed for the messages they are conveying to others. For instance, do the morning announcements over the public address system always start with the scores and heroes and heroines of the most recent sporting event? Is very little time spent at board meetings on curriculum and/or student types of things? Is there seldom a unanimous vote by the board of education? Do negative comments consistently come out of board meetings? Are interoffice memos originating in the superintendent's office usually very directive in nature?

## Ceremonies

If a symbolic event is to be effective, it must be more than a mandatory exercise, it must be viewed as a sacred occasion. This is why graduation exercises should be conducted with pomp and circumstance. Perhaps this is why senior cut days should not be condoned. Ceremonies should say that *something important is being celebrated here*. As with rituals, it is imperative that ceremonies reinforce the core organizational values.

## Storytelling

Historically, cultures have perpetuated themselves through the art of storytelling. Some would say this is becoming a lost art. However, there usually is a cadre of individuals in an organization who are very knowledgeable of the organization's past and interested in sharing it with others. These individuals should be encouraged.

## Cultural network

The cultural network is the informal communication system that tells how things really are within the school system. This network is a true indication of the real core values of a school system. Things cannot be dictated to this system. It disseminates only those things it wants to disseminate and considers important. Therefore, this network must be recognized and nourished with tender loving care. Its transmissions cannot be left purely to chance.

One last way in which organizational culture can be shaped is with the employment of personnel. Because an organizational culture is nothing more than the collective values of its members, it is of utmost importance that new hires share a commitment to the system's core values. In the final analysis, this value commitment could be more important to the system than a 4.0 grade point average in one's teaching area. Too often, very little time is spent ferreting out an individual's value system prior to employment.

## CONCLUDING COMMENTS

Transformational leadership *is* the superintendency. It's having a vision of what the school system can be and motivating all associated with the system to have pride in the system and to achieve more than they thought possible for the good of the system. It is stimulating and releasing the creative energies of all for the benefit of the system.

Transformational leadership is exciting in that while some descriptions can be given of what it is and some general guidelines can be put forth on how to become one, there is no prescription that can be put forth to produce a transformational leader. It is a leadership art as much as a leadership science. It is a school system revitalizing ". . . itself through the combined efforts of its people" (Ruane, 1984).

## REFERENCES

Avolio, B. J., and B. M. Bass (1986). *Transformational Leadership, Charisma, and Beyond*. (Technical Report No. 85-90). Binghamton: State University of New York, School of Management.

Bass, B. M. (1985). *Leadership and Performance Beyond Expectations*. New York: The Free Press.

Bennis, W. G. (1984, August). "The Four Competencies of Leadership." *Training and Development Journal*, pp. 14-19.

Bennis, W., and B. Nanus (1985). *Leaders: The Strategies for Taking Charge*. New York: Harper & Row.

Burns, J. M. (1978). *Leadership*. New York: Harper & Row.

Deal, T. E., and A. Kennedy (1982). *Corporate Cultures: The Rites and Rituals of Corporate Life*. Reading, Mass.: Addison-Wesley.

Deal, T. E. (1985). "The Symbolism of Effective Schools." *The Elementary School Journal*, 85(5), 601-620.

DuFour R., and R. Eaker (1987, September). "The Principal as Leader: Two Major Responsibilities." *NASSP Journal*, pp. 80-89.

Johnston, J. H. (1987). "Values, Culture and the Effective School." *NASSP Journal*, 71, 79-88.

Peters, T. J., and R. H. Waterman (1982). *In Search of Excellence*. New York: Harper & Row.

Ruane, P. (1984). "Moving Through and Beyond Transition: Barriers and Bridges to a Better Quality of Organizational Life." Unpublished doctoral dissertation. Harvard University, Cambridge, Mass.

Schein, E. H. (1987). *Organizational Culture and Leadership*. San Francisco: Jossey-Bass.

Tichy, N. M., and D. O. Ulrich (1984). "The Leadership Challenge—A Call for the Transformational Leader." *Sloan Management Review*, 26(1), 59-68.

Tichy, N. M., and M. A. Devanna (1986). *The Transformational Leader*. New York: John Wiley & Sons.

Wortman, M. S. (1982). "Strategic Management and Changing Leader-Follower Roles." *Journal of Applied Behavioral Science*, 18, 371-383.

# Superintendent Leadership Competencies: Personal (The Superintendent as . . .)

# CHAPTER 8

# The Superintendent as Divergent Thinker

## INTRODUCTION

In the preceding chapter on transformational leadership, the transformational leader was depicted as one who is less willing to be satisfied with partial answers or to accept the status quo. Conversely, this individual is more likely to seek new ways to do things and to take greater risks. The transformational leader is a visionary and an intellectual stimulator. S/he is a leader who provides ideas that result in the rethinking of old ways. S/he enables followers to look at problems from many angles and encourages them to seek creative solutions.

In order to be a transformational leader, one must be a divergent thinker. The Webster's dictionary (1976) definition of divergent is "mov(ing) or extend(ing) in different directions from a common point" (p. 214). In the educational arena, this means challenging commonly held assumptions i.e., all children must spend twelve years in a formal and organized school setting, schools are the primary dispensers of knowledge to youth, etc.

From the time one is very young, emphasis is placed on being right. Young children are encouraged to stay within the lines when coloring and not to draw pink elephants. The entire grading system in grades K-12 and indeed, on through graduate school is predicated on being right. Preparation programs in educational administration stress logical thought processes in problem solving and decision making. Thus, almost all of one's formal educational experiences stress being *right* and the derivation of correct answers through logical thought processes. In other words, *convergent* thinking is emphasized.

When one enters the teaching profession, one is expected to teach a prescribed curriculum and to have a thorough knowledge of one's content area. When one obtains an administrative position, one is expected to apply rational thought processes to the resolution of problems, go through prescribed budget formulation exercises, promote the commonly accepted educational assumptions, and by all means, not suggest wild ideas with any degree of seriousness. The result is that the convergent thinking to which one has been exposed during the formal schooling process is reinforced in the job setting. Now, suddenly, and with no real preparation as a superintendent, one is not only expected to be a *divergent* thinker but also to encourage others to be divergent thinkers.

## THE NEED FOR DIVERGENT THINKING

Divergent thinking is essential to the first two phases of the decision-making process, which are problem definition and idea production; whereas, convergent thinking comes into play during the last three phases of the decision-making process, namely idea evaluation, implementation, and evaluation.

Problem definition, or problem finding, is probably the most neglected phase of decision making. There is a great tendency to assume that one knows the problem and to embark immediately on finding a resolution through the convergent-thinking process; however, a solution to the wrong problem does no one any good and has wasted a lot of time in the process. In the book, *If You Don't Know Where You're Going, You'll Probably End Up Somewhere Else* Campbell (1974) aptly describes the confusion that exists when a problem has not been adequately defined. This confusion can exist in the big picture, such as in strategic planning, as well as in the day-to-day problems faced by superintendents, such as a troublesome board member.

Many of the issues one identifies as difficulties are merely only symptoms of the real problems. For instance, by applying the theories presented in the next chapter on motivation to the collective bargaining process, one should entertain the idea that salaries and fringe benefits are, at times at least, symptoms of teacher discontent in other areas. By bargaining innovatively and attempting to satisfy some esteem needs of teachers, the salary and fringe benefit issues may prove less troublesome to resolve.

In a noneducational example of problem identification, the management of a high-rise hotel was receiving a number of complaints from its guests about having to wait too long for the elevators. Some alternatives that come readily to mind for resolving this perceived problem are to put in another elevator, reprogram the existing elevators, revise the room assignment policies, offer reduced rates for the upper floors, etc. The resolution was very simple and included none of the above: pictures were hung in the elevator waiting areas. In reality, the guests were not having to wait long at all. The problem was that while waiting for the elevator, there was nothing to do but stare at the blank walls, and time passed very slowly in this setting. The old adage that "a watched pot never boils" was very appropriate to this problem. The original ideas listed for resolution were all mechanical or logistical in nature. It was not until someone had the idea that maybe the problem was psychological in origin that the real problem emerged, and along with it, a simple and effective resolution.

The remainder of the chapter discusses some thought processes that must be developed and utilized if one is to become a divergent thinker. Or, applied to the superintendency, if one wishes to be a visionary leader, a leader who wants to identify and deal with *real* problems, and a leader who wants to identify innovative and exciting resolutions to problems, then one must develop divergent-thinking capabilities.

## DEVELOPING DIVERGENT THINKING

Contrary to the thinking of many, creativity or the ability to innovate is not an inherited trait reserved for a fortunate few. While it is true that some individuals are more inclined to search for novel approaches than others, all have the potential to be creative. Interestingly, most individuals when asked to identify something they have done within the last six months that has been innovative will reply that they cannot recall doing anything innovative, and that in general, they just are not the innovative types. However, with some prodding, almost all will be able to identify something they have done that has been innovative. Researchers have generally concluded that a belief in one's ability to be creative is the single most important factor to being creative. To make maximum use of the ideas that follow for developing creative ideas, one must first develop the personal confidence that one does have creative potential.

Novel or innovative ideas do not spring from a vacuum; rather, they come from the novel combination of knowledge and/or experiences stored in one's mind. Creative people know a lot about a lot of things. Roger von Oech (1986) calls this the "explorer" stage. In this stage, one breaks out of routines and looks for new information. He suggests such things as looking in outside fields, looking for lots of ideas (nothing is worthless), and not jumping at the first solution. Campbell (1977) calls this the "experience" stage where one picks up the background to the problem. His book addresses this knowledge-gathering phase. In summary, the components of an innovative idea are not necessarily innovative and novel in and of themselves. What is innovative and novel is the way in which they have been adapted and combined to provide an original solution to a problem.

The idea generation phase is referred to by von Oech as the "artist" stage. This is the off-the-wall stage where one should get a little crazy. Break the rules, do something different, fool around. The greatest danger the artist faces is becoming a prisoner to familiarity. Don't evaluate ideas immediately. Look at a job backwards. (How can one be a less effective superintendent?) Comedy is important; it brings to light the unexpected. Look at the same things as everyone else but come up with new ideas. Campbell (1977) refers to idea generation as the "creativity" phase where individuals develop the ability to give up traditional viewpoints and to veer off the beaten path to explore new and novel things.

Kanter (1986) stresses contact with other individuals who do not share the same values or assumptions. Creativity often flows from uncomfortable situations where basic beliefs are challenged. The most productive research scientists have the most contact with people outside their field because creativity often emerges at the boundaries of disciplines. Outsiders can see the picture a little differently, look at a different angle, and not know enough not to ask the *dumb* question. Kanter calls this "innovation by invasion."

The relationship between comedy and creativity merits special mention. Kanter (1986) indicates that creativity is playfulness and irreverence, and goes on to say:

> Every creative act is a form of play—playing with ideas, twisting the kaleidoscope of reality. Every new invention is a little bit irreverent: it challenges orthodoxy and trods on tradition (p. 12).

Indeed, there is a close connection between *ha-ha* and *a-ha*. Some things are so important that they must be taken lightly and laughed at.

The best way to have good ideas is to have a lot of ideas. One way to do this is through brainstorming. The objective of brainstorming is, in a three- or four-minute period of time, to generate as many ideas as possible. (Shoot for 40 ideas.) Four rules for successful brainstorming are:

1. Criticism of any kind is a no-no.
2. Freewheeling is welcomed. (The wilder the idea the better.)
3. Quantity is wanted. A fast pace should be maintained.
4. Combinations and improvements are sought.

Roger von Oech (1983) has identified ten mental blocks that cripple creative potential. These ten blocks are as follows:

1. The right answer.
2. That's not logical.
3. Follow the rules.
4. Be practical.
5. Avoid ambiguity.
6. To err is wrong.
7. Play is frivolous.
8. That's not my idea.
9. Don't be foolish.
10. I'm not creative.

The next section identifies ways in which these divergent-thinking ideas can be applied to the superintendency.

## APPLICATION OF DIVERSE THINKING TO THE SUPERINTENDENCY

It has been said that professionals today know more and more about less and less. In education, this is reflected by the English teacher who reads only English publications and associates only with other English teachers (perhaps only tenth grade English teachers). Multiply this example by the number of subject areas, grade levels, and administrative positions, and one gets a picture of massive professional isolation.

To combat professional isolationism, educators should be encouraged to do such things as attend seminars in other fields, subscribe to journals in unrelated fields and journals which espouse viewpoints contrary to one's own, and associate with individuals who question the effectiveness of contemporary educational organizations.

Within the school setting, promote cross-disciplinary activities, such as a physics teacher serving on an English textbook adoption or curriculum revision committee, or vice versa. Have a teacher, or teachers, present something of interest in their academic area to the entire staff. This activity can also be done with the administrative staff.

Break routines. Do things differently on occasion for the sole purpose of doing them differently. Use a different format for a meeting and hold it at a different time. If one really wants to get far out, have the custodian, a sixth grader, or a parent run the schools for a day.

Educators, particularly administrators, tend to be serious and dedicated individuals. This demeanor is difficult to fault; however, taken to the extreme, it can have a stifling effect on the school climate and put a damper on creativity. It is important that playful activities be supported within the school system. Otherwise, one cannot expect individuals to be playful when it is important to be playful, i.e., when an innovative approach is needed to a knotty problem such as falling student achievement scores. Halloween parties, gag gift birthday parties, humorous awards, etc. help set the stage for playing over serious business.

To illustrate how difficult it is to poke fun at professional problems, particularly those in which one has a personal stake, divide a group of educators into groups of four or five. Have each group brainstorm for four minutes to identify as many ways as possible to keep bugs off the windshields of cars, and then have them post their ideas. Two things will be noticed. First, during the brainstorming session, there was much laughing and smiles abounded. Second, some rather far-out solutions were identified. These far-out ideas are important because it is ideas like these that lead to other ideas which lead to innovative resolutions. Next, have these same groups brainstorm ideas on an important educational problem, e.g., how would formal K-12 education be affected if the passing of a competency test was all that was needed to obtain a high school diploma? Again, have the ideas posted. Three things will be noticed this time. First, there was much less humor during the brainstorming for this is serious business now. Second, there were some deviations from the brainstorming ground rule of no criticism of ideas. Third, not as many far-out ideas have been generated. It is almost heresy to think, let alone say among colleagues, that the primary function of the schools in the future may be to provide diagnostic and prescriptive services. In fact, it is a good bet that some very obvious possibilities such as schools ceasing to exist and teachers becoming private entrepreneurs commanding pay commensurate to the achievements of their students were not even mentioned.

Lest one think that the above is an idle academic exercise in frivo-
lity, a case can be made for the primary reason that legislatures across
the nation have demanded competency testing for students, teachers,
and administrators is that the education profession ignored, for over
a decade, a serious and growing public concern for an increased
accountability of K-12 educational programs. Instead of identifying
effective and innovative ways to be accountable, educators spent their
time explaining why they couldn't and/or shouldn't be held accountable. After futile attempts to get the education profession to address
this issue, the public felt compelled to address it through their elected
representatives.

Campbell (1977) has identified the following seven characteristics
of creative managers:

*Willing to absorb risks taken by subordinates*: Leaders who
encourage creativity expect that errors will be made. They are able
to accept short-term failures in the hope of achieving long-term
success.

*Comfortable with half-developed ideas*: These leaders don't require
every detail to be in place before accepting an idea. This requires
instinct and judgment on the part of the leaders. Every *half-baked*
idea cannot be pursued.

*Willing to "stretch" company policy*: These leaders don't normally
disregard rules and policies, but they have a *feel* for when the rules
need to be stretched.

*Able to make quick decisions*: These leaders have developed the
ability to recognize when a partially developed idea is worth bet-
ting on without waiting for further studies or committee reports.

*Good listeners*: These leaders seem to have the ability to draw out
the best from their subordinates and then add to it.

*Don't dwell on mistakes*: These leaders are more future oriented
than past oriented. They learn from past mistakes but don't wallow
in them.

*Enjoy their job*: These leaders like what they are doing. They do
not feel trapped. They add energy to their environments.

Being creative is risky. Professionals must feel valued and secure
before they become risk takers. A future chapter is devoted to the
superintendent's role in promoting risk-taking propensity.

Finally, there comes a time when one must become practical and assess the value of an idea and the feasibility of its being successfully implemented. It is obvious that after a decision has been made and time, effort, and money have been spent in its implementation, any drastic changes should not be taken lightly. However, the common mistake is for educational decision makers to become too serious, too logical, and too committed to an idea or resolution too fast.

The best way for a superintendent to get innovation started in his/her district is to lead the way. Positive and helpful innovations emanating from the superintendent's office will not go unnoticed. They need not be grandiose in scale. It is the climate. setting that is important.

In conclusion, the superintendent is paid to be a divergent thinker as well as a convergent thinker; therefore, it is necessary to build divergent thinking time and activities into one's daily calendar. Each Friday one should do a self-analysis of the divergent-thinking time engaged in during the past week.

## REFERENCES

Campbell, D. P. (1977). *Take the Road to Creativity and Get Off Your Dead End.* Greensboro, N.C.: Center for Creative Leadership.

Campbell, D. P. (1974). *If You Don't Know Where You're Going You'll Probably End Up Somewhere Else.* Greensboro, N.C.: Center for Creative Leadership.

Kanter, R. M. (1986, February). "Creating the Creative Environment." *Management Review*, pp. 11-12.

von Oech, R. (1983). *A Whack on the Side of the Head.* New York: Warner Books.

von Oech, R. (1986). *A Kick in the Seat of the Pants.* New York: Harper & Row.

*Webster's Pocket Book Dictionary.* (1976). New York: Simon & Schuster, Inc.

# CHAPTER 9

# The Superintendent as Motivator

## INTRODUCTION

During the last twenty years, the subject of motivation has provided writers and practitioners with fertile ground for research and inquiry. The result has been the emergence of a number of motivation perspectives and models with many of these relating specifically to the child and the classroom. There is a lack of research on motivation as it applies to educational administration, and superintendents, in particular, seem to have been neglected in this area of study.

This chapter presents a discussion of motivational factors that may influence the leadership effectiveness of a superintendent. The goal of the chapter is to heighten awareness among superintendents as to the importance of these factors. However, first a few words on motivation are in order.

## WHAT IS MOTIVATION?

Motivation is difficult to define. The word has no fixed meaning in contemporary psychology and is used in a variety of ways. For example, Hoy and Miskel (1987) define motivation as the "complex forces, drives, needs, tension states, or other mechanisms that start and maintain voluntary activity toward the achievement of personal goals" (p. 176). Another definition notes that motivation is a matter of choices a person makes regarding what one wants to experience or avoid and the amount of effort to be expended in that regard.

Ms. Mary Jane Landry provided the basic material for this chapter. Ms. Landry is president of the board of education in the Kenosha, Wisconsin, Unified Public School District.

Most definitions seem to contain the following three elements:

1. Activating forces are assumed to exist within individuals.
2. Individual behavior is directed toward something.
3. The surrounding environment must reinforce the intensity and direction of individual drives or forces (Hoy and Miskel, 1987).

Theories on motivation, which are as varied as the definitions, attempt to answer frequently asked "why?" questions about human behavior. Why do people work overtime? Why do some people work harder than others? Why doesn't a salary increase improve production? Why doesn't a pupil attend class?

Motivation theory utilizes two basic approaches, content and process, to formulate answers to the "why?" questions. The content approach specifies only those things that motivate behavior, and content theories attempt to identify what things energize or initiate behavior. Theories in this group list specific needs, motives, expectancies, incentives, goals, and reinforcers.

Process theories investigate how behavior is started, sustained, and stopped. These theories attempt not only to define the major variables that are necessary to explain choice, effort, and the persistence of certain behavior, but also how the variables interact to influence outcomes (Miskel, 1982).

While research on motivation produces a number of definitions, theories, and perspectives, one concept emerges very clearly: the importance of motivation in the workplace is not a new issue. In fact, the principles of motivation have been primary concerns in business administration management ever since the realization that employee motivation has a bearing on productivity (Pastor and Erlandson, 1982). The classic Hawthorne studies, conducted from 1927 to 1932, yielded a number of conclusions that remain important today.

In recent years, an increased interest in motivation has emerged within the educational community. A possible reason for this heightened interest might be found in the report, *A Nation At Risk*. The report focused on the problems facing American public education and stressed the serious lack of motivation for both students and teachers.

Some of the recommendations of the report center around the need to increase teachers' salaries. However, the National Commission on Excellence in Education (1988) also refers to the need to "make teaching a more rewarding and respected profession" (p.30), implying that there is more to motivation than just money. One of the conclusions of the Hawthorne study notes that economic incentives are not the only significant motivators (Hoy and Miskel, 1987).

For whatever reason, motivation in the educational setting has become an area of increased interest among researchers and educators. Superintendents need to be aware of the motivational research and recognize its significance not only within the school organization, but also in the community at large.

## SUPERINTENDENTS AND MOTIVATION

According to Hoy and Miskel (1987), school superintendents need to be aware of the importance of motivation within the educational organization and the teaching profession. A solid understanding of motivation is essential for explaining causes of behavior in schools or divisions, predicting effects of executive decisions, and directing behavior to achieve system goals.

Superintendents need to know how to motivate. If the superintendent is to be a *strong leader*, s/he must be able to motivate other administrators, teachers, parents, students, and the community. Effective leaders don't do the jobs themselves; rather, they motivate others to accomplish the goals of the organization. Patricia Duttweiler (1986) states: "Education excellence requires a leader who has the ability to gain the commitment of others to organizational goals" (p. 371). Thomas McDaniels (1983) indicates that while personal dynamism, wisdom, and decisiveness are all important qualities to possess, the ability to motivate others is a more important factor in reaching school goals.

In his article on motivation, McDaniels presents a number of leadership qualities that relate to motivation. He bases his outline of motivating qualities on research ranging from Elton Mayo's Hawthorne studies to Ouchi's Theory Z. While he relates the qualities to principals and effective schools, the qualities he identifies are equally applicable to superintendents.

If a superintendent is to motivate others, s/he must have a personal commitment to the importance of motivation. This individual must understand that the superintendent's enthusiasm for the goals of the system sets the tone for the system climate. Superintendents motivate others by personal example and believe that motivation is an integral part of the superintendency (McDaniels, 1983).

Another leadership factor that influences motivation is the ability of the chief administrator to involve people, both board and staff, in goal setting and decision making. Much of the research in this area involves teacher motivation and suggests that part of the solution to the problem of motivating teachers lies in involving staff in making decisions that have a direct impact on their work.

The second Gallup/Phi Delta Kappa Poll of Teachers' Attitudes toward the Public Schools conducted in 1989 indicates that teachers don't believe they have the authority they need. They are convinced that they do not have enough control over such vital aspects of instruction as setting discipline policies for their schools, establishing grading policies, and determining academic standards (Elam, 1989).

Jack Frymier (1987) refers to "neutered" teachers as teachers who lack physical strength and energy, enthusiasm for their work, and motivation. He believes that teachers need to be empowered and included in the decisions that affect their work.

Superintendents need to be aware of the importance of sharing decision making at all levels—not just in the classroom. State, system, school, and student levels must also be taken into consideration when delegating authority and decisions.

Another factor to be considered is the significance of the decisions. Centralizing routine decisions and decentralizing significant decisions maximizes participants' motivation (Frymier, 1987). A superintendent needs to identify which decisions are significant and which are routine at each level of the educational organization.

According to Duttweiler (1986), including employees in making decisions in their system will result in an increased sense of ownership in the results of those decisions. Job satisfaction will increase and employees will be motivated to support decisions they have helped make. The superintendent will find that s/he has less work, fewer staff problems, and a smoother operating system.

In addition to involving staff and the community in decision making, a superintendent also needs to be aware of the importance of encouragement and compliments as motivating factors (McDaniels, 1983). It is essential that praise as well as power be shared.

A superintendent, as a motivator, tries to match jobs to individual needs, interests, and talents (McDaniels, 1983). This takes time because it requires a superintendent to personally get to know many people in the system and community. In small communities, this is a fairly easy task; however, in larger communities, the superintendent will have to concentrate on key people and encourage them to identify their employees' needs, interests, and talents.

The result of such effort will benefit both parties. Employees will be set up for success on the job and will find assignments satisfying and rewarding. The superintendent will develop an extensive pool of resources upon which s/he may draw for advice and assistance.

In addition, the superintendent will be knowledgeable about incentives meaningful to system employees. Incentives build interest and satisfy needs. Research indicates that if the needs that motivate an individual to work are satisfied by the organization's incentives, job satisfaction is high. If an individual's needs are greater than the rewards received for work, a discrepancy exists that leads to dissatisfaction (Hoy and Miskel, 1987). Thus, it would seem logical that superintendents who can match incentives with employee needs will be better able to motivate staff.

Not only do the system's internal groups require motivation but external groups do as well. Community business leaders need motivated to become involved with education and understand the importance of the future work force. Parents need to be motivated to become involved with their children's education. Nonparents, particularly senior citizens, need to be motivated to utilize educational services and understand the changes and functions of today's educational process. Taxpayers need to be motivated to support the educational investment. Legislators need to be motivated to provide continued legal and statutory support for the overall educational enterprise. In essence, every element of the community needs to be motivated to provide the best possible education for each and every child.

Finally, the superintendent needs to set high expectations for self, staff, and students. S/he must be confident in the capabilities of her/his staff to meet those expectations and the organization's goals.

## THE APPLICATION OF MOTIVATION THEORY: AN EXAMPLE

In the preceding section, the importance of the superintendent serving as a motivational leader was discussed. In addition, motivational tips drawn from the motivational literature were presented. This section provides an example of the practical application of two motivational theories to the superintendency setting.

The superintendent must continually assess the personal needs of the system's administrators and teachers. In this assessment process, the work of Maslow and Herzberg (Hersey and Blanchard, 1982) can be used as a basis of operation. In Maslow, the lower order needs of security and affiliation must be satisfied before any real work can begin on raising employee productivity levels. This can be accomplished by the superintendent through the provision of appropriate remuneration, stability in employment, serving as a buffer with special interest groups, and by practicing team management. Once these lower order (or deficit) needs are fulfilled, the needs of individuals will move to the esteem and self-actualization (growth) levels. At these levels, professionalism assumes a paramount role, and the potential for increasing employee productivity is present.

Herzberg built upon Maslow's theory. He refers to the lower order needs as hygiene factors and indicates that these factors, comprising working conditions, interpersonal relations, money, status, and security must be satisfied before it is possible to consider raising productivity levels. The satisfaction of these factors keeps productivity from decreasing but does not increase it. In order to increase productivity, the staff must be moved to the level where their needs fall within what Herzberg refers to as the "motivators" category, which is equivalent to the esteem and self-actualization levels of Maslow. "Motivators" consist of such things as recognition for accomplishment, challenging work, increased responsibility, and personal growth and development. The ways in which a superintendent can address these needs are limited only by one's imagination and ability to effectively match motivators to the needs of employees.

## CONCLUDING COMMENTS

Motivating others to work toward the accomplishment of organizational goals is the essence of leadership. It is interesting that motivational theories are rather straight-forward and easy to apply but are often ignored by leaders. Hopefully, this chapter has made a case not only for the importance of motivation in the life of the superintendent but also for the study and on-the-job application of relevant motivational theories.

The next chapter on "Assessing and Altering Risk-Taking Propensity" builds upon the motivational base established in this chapter.

## REFERENCES

Duttweiler, P. C. (1986). "Educational Excellence and Motivating Teachers." *The Clearing House*, *59*, 371-374.

Elam, S. M. (1989, June). "The Second Gallup/Phi Delta Kappa Poll of Teachers' Attitudes Toward the Public Schools." *Phi Delta Kappan*, *70*, pp. 785-798.

Frymier, J. (1987, September). "Bureaucracy and the Neutering of Teachers." *Phi Delta Kappan*, *69*, p. 914.

Hersey, P., and K. Blanchard (1982). *Management of Organizational Behavior*. Englewood Cliffs, N.J.: Prentice-Hall, Inc.

Hoy, W. K., and C. G. Miskel (1987). *Educational Administration: Theory Research and Practice*. New York: Random House.

McDaniels, T. (1983). "The Principal as Motivator: Effective Schools, Theory Z, and Leadership Style." *American Secondary Education*, *13*(11), 18-20.

Miskel, C. G. (1982, Summer). "Motivation in Educational Organizations." *Educational Administration Quarterly*, *18*(3), pp. 65-88.

National Commission on Excellence in Education (1983). *A Nation at Risk: The Imperative for Educational Reform*. Washington D.C.: National Commission on Excellence in Education.

Pastor, M. C., and D. A. Erlandson (1982). "A Study of Higher Order Need Strength and Job Satisfaction in Secondary School Teachers." *The Journal of Educational Administration*, *18*(2), 172-183.

# CHAPTER 10

# The Superintendent as Assessor and Alterer of Risk-Taking Propensity

The ability to make and successfully implement effective decisions is the stock and trade of the successful leader. However, despite the best intentions and decision-making skills of the leader, the outcomes of decisions are never entirely predictable. The element of risk is always present in varying degrees. Some decision makers prefer to minimize risk taking by relying upon a bureaucracy in which personal choices, value judgments, and individual motivations are minimized. Others are motivated and have fashioned a career by *living on the edge*. Thus, it is obvious that decision makers vary in their propensity to engage in risk-taking behavior.

Effective decision making is a product of both the quality of the decision and the degree to which it is accepted by those upon whom it impacts. Much has been written about the processes by which decisions are made and the strategies that can be used in their implementation. In these writings, the role that risk-taking propensity plays in the decision and its implementation is seldom mentioned; however, risk-taking propensity can and does significantly influence both components of effective decisionmaking. For instance, risk-taking propensity will have a direct bearing on a superintendent's decision as to whether, or how, to address the situation of a very successful high school football coach who is also a very poor and uninspired teacher. If the superintendent's motivation is to keep community conflict to a minimum, then a decision probably will be made to look the other way, for his/her risk-taking propensity will be low. If, on the other

This chapter was adopted from an article written by William Konnert and Bradley Garner entitled "Assessing and Altering Risk-Taking Propensity: Keys to Superintendency Success" that appeared in the Spring, 1987 edition of *Catalyst for Change*.

hand, student academic achievement, student time on task, etc. are uppermost on the superintendent's agenda, then personal risk-taking propensity may be greater, and the superintendent may decide to directly address the problem.

Regardless of the decision made in the above example, it probably has little chance of success if the high school administrators are not personally committed to the decision and share the perceived risk. If they assume a commitment to the decisions, they too must have a high risk-taking propensity. Thus, it becomes incumbent upon a superintendent to assess both personal risk-taking propensity as well as that of significant others in a given situation. Further, it is imperative that the superintendent not only know how to assess both personal risk-taking propensity and that of others, but also that this individual know how to alter it when necessary.

## ASSESSING RISK-TAKING PROPENSITY

For the purposes of this discussion, the term *risk* will be used to refer to the likelihood of negative consequences as the direct result of an administrative decision. Thus, *propensity for risk taking* refers to the tendency of an administrator to make and implement a decision in which the potential for negative consequences is relatively high. (Hopefully the potential payoff is equally as high.)

Assessing the risk-taking propensity of individuals involved in a particular situation involves an assessment of the risk-taking propensity of each individual as well as an assessment of the prevailing organizational climate. In assessing the risk-taking propensity of individuals, one must first assess their motives. For example, achievement, power, and affiliation are viewed as three powerful motives (McClelland et al., 1953). Thus, individuals with a high need for *achievement* will tend to set personal goals of low or intermediate difficulty in order to assure a high likelihood of success. Risk-taking propensity in these individuals will tend to be relatively low. As an example, a *split board*, which typically fosters a climate in which the security and continuity of administrators is tenuous, often promotes a climate of low risk-taking propensity. On the other hand, individuals with a *power* motive probably will tend to take greater risks to achieve their ends. *Affiliation*, or the need to be liked by others, results in a very low risk-taking propensity. It is doubtful whether administrators with a high need for affiliation can be successful in a collective bargaining environment or in other situations requiring confrontation.

Incentives and expectancy are two other factors that affect risk-taking propensity. *Incentives* are described by Atkinson (1957) as the ". . . relative attractiveness of a specific goal that is offered in a situation or the relative unattractiveness of an event that might occur as the consequence of some act" (p. 360). Thus, it is obvious that an individual's incentives are directly linked to his/her personal motivations. *Expectancy* is the ". . . cognitive anticipation . . . that performance of some act will be followed by a particular consequence" (p. 360). Expectancy is assessed by relating the anticipated outcome of implementing a decision with the degree to which the perceived outcome will fulfill personal motives.

The degrees of importance attached to motives, incentives, and expectancies are relative; however, motives will probably receive the highest weighting (because incentives and expectancies are assessed in relation to the degree to which they are likely to satisfy personal motives).

In summary, it can be said that personal propensity for risk taking is an interaction of motives, incentives, and expectancies. While there are specific ways in which individual motives, incentives, and expectancies can be derived, the net effect of the interaction of these three factors must still remain as only an estimation. Thus, there is a considerable amount of subjectivity associated with the assessment of risk-taking propensity, and to a degree then, its appropriate assessment remains an administrative art. However, a cognizance of and attention to these factors help to direct the leader's attention to the proper issues and in so doing, decrease the randomness of assessment.

A study by Brown (1970) investigated the differences in risk-taking propensity between business and public school administrators. The results indicated that business administrators are *more willing* to take risks regardless of age, experience, or the size of the organization. Brown concluded that business and public school administrators may indeed have the same innate ability to take risks during the decision-making process. The differences in risk-taking propensity, according to Brown, may be a function of organizational climate. It is hypothesized that perceptions of personnel instability, political considerations, and the influence of external constituencies are three important factors that impact upon the organizational climate in the public schools and lower the risk-taking propensity of administrators. Thus, an assessment of working conditions is also crucial to the assessment of risk-taking propensity of individuals within the system.

While individual and organizational factors affecting risk-taking propensity have been presented separately, in reality, risk taking is a function of individual motivations coupled with the interaction of the leader in his/her working environment. Both factors must be taken into consideration by the superintendent in attempts to assess, and subsequently alter, risk-taking propensity.

## ALTERING RISK-TAKING PROPENSITY

In an effort to increase decision-making quality and the effectiveness of policy implementation within a school system, it is necessary at times for the superintendent to alter the risk-taking propensity of individuals within the system. While it is possible that the superintendent might feel a need to decrease risk-taking propensity, it is far more likely that an increase will be sought, for most significant decisions with a high payoff potential also involve a high element of risk. Therefore, this section will specifically address ways in which the superintendent can foster increased risk-taking propensity.

The two most significant factors are that the superintendent must be secure in the position and enjoy full support from the board of education. Insecurity at the top of an organization makes for low risk-taking propensity within the organization. With security and support, the superintendent assumes position power, is in a position to assume a leadership role, and can reward risk taking.

The superintendent must also be perceived as one who is going to remain in the position for a *reasonable* period of time. If the superintendent is perceived in this manner, it will be assumed by the staff that this individual will be around to share in the responsibility of the decisions initiated. The top leader in the organization must not be viewed as a hit-and-run artist who makes a big splash and then leaves others to put the pieces together. Likewise, the staff will be much less likely to take the attitude that if they can ride things out for a couple of years the superintendent will leave and they can revert back to their old ways. Unfortunately, the risk-enhancing factors discussed in the preceding two paragraphs are not present in many systems today. Perhaps this is why public education has often been accused of lacking direction.

The superintendent must be viewed as one who is politically astute, but also one who is honest and will persevere when the going gets tough. This individual must be receptive and sensitive to the concerns of external constituencies, but also must steer a straight path and not be subject to the whims of the most persistent or vocal special interest group.

The superintendent must move from the power and leadership bases described above to establish an organizational climate that is conducive to a high risk-taking propensity. This can be done by being supportive of risk taking and by tolerating mistakes and *sticking with* those who make them. In short, a climate that says "Change is O.K." and is, in fact, encouraged and valued must be fostered.

## CONCLUDING COMMENTS

It is important that the element of risk not become the overriding factor in educational decision making. A high risk-taking propensity tends to lessen the fear of risk, thereby keeping the risk element in perspective so that the educational elements can receive their appropriate consideration in the decision-making process. Once a decision has been reached, its implementation is much more likely to be successful if those responsible are committed to it and have a high risk-taking propensity and *go-for-it* attitude.

This discussion has attempted to make suggestions for assessing and altering risk-taking propensity that are practical, workable, and solidly grounded in theory. Their application should enhance education in a school system by serving as a vital supplement to sound decision making and implementation strategies.

## REFERENCES

Allison, G. T. (1969). "Conceptual Models and the Cuban Missile Crisis." *The American Political Science Review*, *69*(3), 689-718.

Atkinson, J. W. (1957). "Motivational Determinants of Risk-Taking Behavior." *Psychological Review*, *64*, 359-372.

Brown, J. S. (1970). "Risk Propensity in Decision Making: A Comparison of Business and Public School Administrators." *Administrative Science Quarterly*, *15*(4), 473-481.

Campbell, R. F., J. E. Corbally and R. O. Nystrand (1983). *Introduction to Educational Administration*. Boston: Allyn & Bacon.

Eklund, E. (1977). "Promoting Change Through Systems Advocacy." In L. D. Baucom and G. J. Bensberg (Eds.), *Advocacy Systems for Persons With Developmental Disabilities* (pp. 177-184). Lubbock, TX: Research and Training Center in Mental Retardation, Texas Tech Univ.

Hersey, P. and K. Blanchard (1982). *Management of Organizational Behavior*. Englewood Cliffs, N.J.: Prentice-Hall, Inc.

Holloway, W. H. and G. A. Niazi (1978). "A Study of Leadership Style, Situation Favorableness, and the Risk-Taking Behaviors of Leaders." *Journal of Educational Administration*, *16*(2), 160-168.

Kogan, N. and M. A. Wallach (1964). *Risk Taking: A Study in Cognition and Personality*. New York: Holt, Rinehart, & Winston.

Kogan, N., M. A. Wallach and R. B. Burt (1968). "Are Risk-Takers More Persuasive than Conservatives in a Group Discussion?" *Journal of Experimental Psychology*, *4*(1), 76-88.

McClelland, D. C., J. W. Atkinson, R. A. Clark and E. L. Lowell (1953). *The Achievement Motive*. New York: Appleton-Century-Crofts.

McClelland, D. C. and R. I. Watson (1973). "Power Motivation and Risk-Taking Behavior." *Journal of Personality*, *41*, 121-139.

McClelland, D. C. and R. I. Watson (1975). "Predicting Risk Preference Among Power-Related Tasks." *Journal of Personality*, *43*, 266-285.

Miller, N. E. and J. Dollard (1941). *Social Learning and Imitation*. New Haven, CT: Yale Univ. Press.

O'Brien, R. H., M. Clarke and S. Kamieniecki (1984). "Open and Closed Systems of Decision Making: The Case of Toxic Waste Management." *Public Administration Review*, *44*(4), 334-352.

Weber, M. (1980). "The Three Types of Legitimate Rule." In A. Etzioni and E. W. Lehman (Eds.), *A Sociological Reader on Complex Organizations* (pp. 4-10). New York: Holt, Rinehart, & Winston.

# CHAPTER 11

# The Superintendent as Empowerer

Empowerment is the vehicle through which transformational leadership is achieved. It is the key by which a superintendent is able to create and maintain a strong and consistent desire for excellence within his/her system.

Thus, the role of the superintendent in empowering others is the focus of this chapter. The chapter is divided into three sections. The first section provides a definition of empowerment and explores the relationship between empowerment and leadership—the what of the superintendent and empowerment. The second section examines the groups to be empowered—the who of the superintendent and empowerment. The final section focuses on empowerment skills and practices—the how of the superintendent and empowerment.

## EMPOWERMENT DEFINITION AND LEADERSHIP (the *what* of empowerment)

### Definition

The word *empower* means *to give power*. Power can be understood as a coercive force or the imposition of ideas or authority. In this context, it becomes synonymous with control and dominance. This is a legitimate understanding of power but it is not the meaning of empowerment.

Dr. Jack Calareso provided the basic material for this chapter. Dr. Calareso is an assistant professor at College of St. Rose in Albany, New York. He was formerly the superintendent of schools in the Diocese of Green Bay, Wisc. He recently has completed extensive research in the empowerment area.

Empowerment is *power sharing*. As such, it encourages people ". . . to be involved in decision making . . . engenders increased commitment . . . self-respect . . . and satisfaction . . ." (Stimson and Appelbaum, 1988, p. 314). Empowerment is leadership that provides autonomy, responsibility and freedom. It creates the environment for commitment, dedication, and the realistic accomplishment of mutually understood and accepted goals. It allows for a common vision, shared values, and mutual respect.

In the educational arena, empowerment is "a deliberate effort to provide . . . the room, right, responsibility, and resources to make sensible decisions and informed professional judgments . . ." (Sergiovanni, 1989a, p. 5). Lest this be confused with a directionless free-for-all, empowerment in education includes acceptance of "responsibility to achieve" along with "responsibility to decide" (p. 6). Goals, objectives, and standards do exist. With empowered leadership, however, the commitment and direction are commonly developed and shared with mutual accountability.

Furthermore, the understanding of empowerment must always balance rights and duty (Bloom, 1987). With every right given to an educational leader (principal, teacher, board member, parent, etc.) there exists a clear and corresponding duty. The decisions made and actions taken must reflect what is right and good for the students and their educational experience.

Power sharing by superintendents is "power investment" (Sergiovanni, 1989b, p. 220). Leadership by empowerment brings more power back to the superintendent, however, this increased power is not a domination of people and resources. Rather, it is measured by growth, success, and accomplishments of the educational system. Increased power is reflected by efficiency, efficacy, and creativity. "Empowered individuals feel alive . . . and become part of a community with a common purpose" (Lagana, 1989). Perhaps most importantly, students learn, achieve, and develop to their full potential.

## Leadership

Leadership is a process that brings about the accomplishment of goals. The methodologies of leadership are influence, authority, and/or power.

Leadership is critical to excellence. What is most important, however, is the style or philosophy of leadership that permeates the superintendent's actions.

Burns' (1978) definition of leadership as an act that induces "followers to act for certain goals that represent the values . . . of both leaders and followers" (p. 19) provides a basis for understanding of the superintendent as leader. Transformative leadership unites the superintendent with the principals, board, and others through a common goal and level of commitment that "raises one another to higher levels of motivation and morality" (p. 20). It is this understanding of leadership that is called empowerment, and the most efficacious leadership style for the superintendent is leadership by empowerment.

## EMPOWERED GROUPS (the *who* of empowerment)

It is necessary to understand the scope of the superintendent's empowering relationships. Although time and attention devoted to one empowered group may be disproportionate to that devoted to others, the effectiveness of the school system depends on the empowerment of all the partners in the educational endeavor. An image that helps represent this shared responsibility and relationship is the wheel. The superintendent is the hub with the *spokes of empowerment* connected to each group involved in the system. Carrying the analogy one step further, an efficient vehicle depends on the proper functioning of every wheel. The superintendent leads through empowerment that drives the system to reach its goals. The superintendent provides the power to empower.

### Board of Education

The district's board ideally provides the vision and leadership for the system. Through its development of policies and guidelines, the adoption of a budget, and its public expression of the quality of education, the board influences the limits and perception of the endeavor. An effective board is an empowered board.

The superintendent assists in setting the board's agenda, recommends policy and leadership actions, and facilitates the implementation and evaluation of policy (Ziegler et al., 1985). The superintendent empowers the board to enable effective vision and leadership to develop and flourish.

## Central Office Personnel

While numbers, titles, and position descriptions may vary, central office personnel constitute the superintendent's leadership team. They often represent the superintendent to the schools and community. They play a critical role in the support, resourcing, and implementation of the system's goals and programs. To the degree that these personnel are empowered to achieve the goals of the system, the superintendent and educational community are well served.

## School Principals and Staff

The efficiency of empowerment is very dependent on the superintendent's direct relationship with school principals and indirectly with teachers, aides, and staff. Although a system should strive for common goals and values, the place of education is the school. It is the school that has the greatest potential to be effective and excellent.

Excellent schools are led by excellent principals. Excellent principals are leaders by empowerment, and it is the superintendent who empowers the principals.

The school principal then must empower his/her staff because these individuals articulate the vision and mission into a dynamic curriculum.

## Teachers' Union

While many participate in the negotiation of collective bargaining agreements, it is through this relationship with the teachers' union that the superintendent directly *leads* the teachers. The superintendent has the opportunity to empower the teachers and their representatives through open and equitable negotiations and dialogue.

## Parents and Community

Empowerment of parents and the community at large is more than public relations, it is a call to participation. Parents are the primary educators of their children. The community is the primary supporter of the system and the ultimate beneficiary of its efficacy. While schools have received recent criticism from the public (Carnegie Report, Gallup Poll, etc.), there is also a renewed recognition of the necessary partnership between the community and the school.

Superintendents play a significant role in empowering school leaders to actively initiate parent/community programs and efforts. Superintendents must also empower the community to realize its critical role in the educational system. Parents/community are an equally important *wheel* as the educational system moves toward the accomplishment of its goals. The superintendent is the agent of empowerment, and through empowering leadership, the partnership is created, strengthened, and nurtured.

## EMPOWERMENT SKILLS AND PRACTICES (the *how* of empowerment)

In his book, *Thriving on Chaos*, Peters (1987) frequently makes reference to the axiom—there are no limits to the ability to contribute on the part of a properly selected, well-trained, appropriately supported, and, above all, committed person. Empowered school personnel (principals, teachers, board members, central office staff, parents, citizens) have unlimited potential to positively effect the quality of education. The effective superintendent must devote the time and energy necessary to develop the skills and practices of empowerment. Each is integral to the transforming style of leadership that leads to commitment and dedication of the educational partners. A discussion of required skills and practices follows.

### Recruitment and Selection

The axiom alluded to above makes reference to proper selection. It should not be presumed that empowerment is of itself a guarantee of excellence. The people with whom the superintendent interacts must be competent, professional, open, and creative: they must be people who are energized by freedom, responsibility, and participation and must be people who believe in leadership by empowerment.

The superintendent has significant responsibility for his/her staff, school principals, and teachers. Attention must be taken to build a team of capable educators. This may require some difficult personnel decisions and changes. The superintendent has far less input regarding board members and the community. However, it is important to carefully seek out and involve those individuals with the greatest ability to contribute to the team effort.

## Vision and Goals

The articulation of a vision and goals may be the cornerstone of empowerment for the superintendent and the entire educational community. A vision is a statement of belief. It is a core statement of philosophy and values. Goals are specific objectives necessary to embody the vision. They are tangible actions that if enacted will lead to a real feeling of accomplishment and fulfillment.

The need for vision and goals must be understood in terms of the empowering superintendent and the empowered educational partners. The effective superintendent must "develop and live an enabling and empowering vision" (Peters, 1987, p. 283). Clarity of educational vision and frequent articulation of goals create the atmosphere for growth and development.

However, the vision and goals must be owned by everyone. Therefore, while the superintendent must articulate his/her values and philosophy, there must be room for adaptation and change. There must also be a process of interaction leading to a mutually acceptable and shared vision and goals. At this point, everyone becomes empowered to proclaim the vision boldly and loudly.

Finally, this vision and these goals can then become the criteria for evaluation and the substance of celebration. The reality of the vision in the lives of students and the educational community and the successful accomplishment of the educational goals will be both the sign and the experience of an empowered educational system.

## Communication

The ability to communicate one's vision and goals is only a single dimension of the communications area. It is certainly necessary for the effective superintendent to be able to speak clearly, convincingly, and constantly on behalf of the educational mission. Communications has, however, two other dimensions in addition to *output*.

Empowerment also requires the ability to listen (input). The superintendent must not only be able to listen but also able to create both the atmosphere and opportunities for listening to take place. Empowered people believe in and experience openness and attentiveness from their peers and leaders. Their ideas and feelings must not only be heard but acted upon. The superintendent must be available to the educational community in situations that encourage the exchange of ideas and emotions.

The third dimension of communications is networking or facilitation. As depicted earlier, the superintendent is the hub of the wheel. S/he must connect the various dimensions of the educational system to ensure a cohesive and cooperative effort.

Some would assert that there is a serious problem in the loosely coupled structure of school systems. While local schools make responsible decisions (a goal of empowerment), they often lack the connection with other dimensions of the system necessary to make the decisions effective. The necessary facilitation or networking is the responsibility of the superintendent. S/he is the link between the schools, the board, the community, etc.

## Training and Resources

Empowered people need the ongoing opportunity to learn, to develop their skills, and to grow. More importantly, an effect of empowerment will be the desire for training. It will be a manifestation of the commitment of the system and a response to the freedom and responsibility. Training opportunities must be frequent, high quality, and pertinent to the vision and goals.

The need for resources speaks to the availability of materials and personnel (human resources) necessary to successfully achieve the goals. It also refers to compensation and rewards that motivate, affirm, and recognize commitment and excellence.

## Delegation

Implicit in the philosophy of empowerment is the enablement of others and the provision of freedom and responsibility. Individual schools and educational groups must be freed to make their own decisions and to implement the common goals. Decentralization of authority must be real. Delegation by the superintendent will create trust, respect, and confidence and will also help develop effective leadership skills at the local level.

Each dimension of the educational system must fully experience its unique role and responsibility. While accountability always remains, freedom and autonomy are integral to real empowerment. Again the image is the wheel. The superintendent is not at the top of a hierarchical structure; rather, s/he is at the center of a system that moves cooperatively toward the common goal of excellence.

**Atmosphere and Environment**

Implicit in many of the empowerment skills and practices is the atmosphere of freedom and responsibility. The superintendent must create an environment that encourages and nurtures cooperation, commitment, and creativity. Members of the school community must work together. Empowerment must breed commitment and dedication to the vision and goals. There must be active participation and a sense of ownership. This is the necessary *culture* of the effective school system.

**Presence and Example**

Finally, the superintendent can only empower others if s/he also is an empowered leader. The superintendent must lead by example. An effective superintendent practices what s/he promotes. Each day, the superintendent must be about the business of empowering and must present the image of an empowered leader.

Though perhaps a radical concept, the empowering superintendent might be a more effective leader without an office. His/her office should be the classrooms and corridors of the schools, the homes and meeting places of the community, the board room, and the playgrounds. After all, it is the people who are empowered. The superintendent must be visible to and interact with the people of the educational system and in doing so, must constantly exercise his/her empowering power.

**SUMMARY**

Empowerment is transformational leadership in action. It is power sharing. It provides freedom, responsibility, and opportunity to fully participate in the vision and goals of the system. It enables those empowered to experience personal fulfillment, and, most importantly, it leads to excellence in education.

In a school system, the superintendent is the key empowering agent. S/he relates to the central office staff, principals, teachers, board members, and the community at large. S/he serves as the hub of the educational wheel, connecting the educational partners with the spokes of empowerment.

The empowering superintendent believes in the limitless potential of the people in the system. S/he empowers them to reach their potential and make their greatest contributions.

The superintendent carefully recruits and selects personnel who are competent, professional, open, and creative—people who are energized by his/her empowering leadership. The superintendent articulates a clear vision and goals. Empowering leadership allows all participants to own and celebrate this common vision and goals.

Critical empowering skills also include communications (speaking, listening, and networking), training and resources, delegation, and the creation of an atmosphere that encourages and nurtures cooperation, commitment, creativity and risk taking. Empowerment directs all energy toward excellence.

The superintendent is the empowering leader and the empowered model. His/her presence and example witness to the reality that empowerment is not a strategy but a philosophy—a way of life. The superintendent has the power to empower, and the system has the *empower* to achieve excellence.

## REFERENCES

Bloom, A. (1987). *The Closing of the American Mind*. New York, NY: Simon & Schuster.

Burns, J. M. (1978). *Leadership*. New York, NY: Harper & Row.

Gallup, A. M. and D. L. Clark (1987). "The 19th Annual Gallup Poll of the Public's Attitude Toward the Public Schools." *Phi Delta Kappan*, 68(1), 17-30.

Lagana, J. F. (1989). "Ready, Set, Empower! Superintendents Can Sow the Seeds for Growth." *The School Administrator*, 46(1), 20-22.

Peters, T. (1987). *Thriving on Chaos: Handbook for a Management Revolution*. New York: Alfred Knopf.

Sergiovanni, T. J. (1989a). "What Really Counts in Improving Schools?" In Thomas J. Sergiovanni and John H. Moore (Eds.), *Schooling for Tomorrow: Directing Reforms to Issues that Count*. Boston, Mass.: Allyn & Bacon.

Sergiovanni, T. J. (1989b). "The Leadership Needed for a Quality School." In Thomas J. Sergiovanni and John H. Moore (Eds.), *Schooling for Tomorrow: Directing Reforms to Issues that Count*. Boston, Mass.: Allyn & Bacon.

Stimson, T. D. and R. P. Appelbaum (1988). "Empowering Teachers: Do Principals Have the Power?." *Phi Delta Kappan*, *69*(4), 313-316.

*Task Force on Teaching as a Profession, a Nation Prepared: Teachers for the 21st Century* (1987). Washington DC: Carnegie Foundation.

Zeigler, H., E. Kehoe and J. Reilsman (1985). *City Managers and School Superintendents*. New York, NY: Praeger.

# Superintendent Leadership Competencies: Professional (The Superintendent as . . .)

# CHAPTER 12

# The Superintendent as the Board's Chief Executive Officer

Successful superintendents must never forget that they are employees of the board of education. As such, the board of education is the boss.

The neglect of the simple truism stated above probably has been responsible for more superintendents losing their jobs than any other single cause. When a superintendent begins to think that because one has spent a number of years in preparation for the superintendency, and thus, is eminently more qualified to determine the fate of the school district than a small group of noneducators, the road becomes steep and usually ends abruptly. When one begins to view the system as one's personal possession, the beginning of the end has begun.

If any complex organization is going to be effective in setting and achieving meaningful goals, the board of directors and the chief executive officer (CEO) must work well together. The board collectively and board members individually must have trust and confidence in the CEO. When this board/CEO relationship sours and when trust and confidence wane, the CEO is soon looking for another job.

Mr. Craig Gifford and Mr. Thomas Dickson, executive vice president and director of educational services respectively, of the Ohio School Boards Association provided the basic material for the section on "Board Expectations of the Superintendent." Mr. Gifford has served on a city board of education for eight years. He also has had experiences as a central office administrator in the Columbus, Ohio, City Schools and as a newspaper editor. Prior to joining the staff of the Ohio School Boards Association, Mr. Dickson was a superintendent of schools. He also has served as an assistant superintendent and as a high school principal.

Mr. Conrad Ott provided the basic information for the section on "Working with the Board of Education." Mr. Ott has served as superintendent of the Akron, Ohio, City Schools for the past twenty-three years. This makes him the dean of city superintendents in the nation. During this time, he has never had a recommendation to the board defeated.

The effectiveness one will experience as the top educational leader in the school system, the job satisfaction one will derive, and in the final analysis, one's longevity in the superintendency will be determined by the extent to which one is able to build and maintain a strong relationship with the board of education. Therefore, this chapter on the superintendent as the chief executive officer of the board presents and discusses information that is extremely important to the professional well-being of anyone sitting in, or aspiring to sit in, the superintendent's chair.

In order to build a strong relationship with the board, one must know what the board expects of its superintendent. While there will be some variation between and among individual boards, certain common expectations of the superintendent that are shared by most board members can be identified.

The next section of this chapter identifies and discusses some commonly accepted board expectations of the superintendent and is followed by some insights into things superintendents can do to help develop and maintain strong relationships with their boards.

## BOARD EXPECTATIONS OF THE SUPERINTENDENT

### Personal Traits

No board will employ a superintendent unless s/he is perceived as an individual who has integrity and courage and is honest, fair, and open. Gaining a reputation as one who possesses these traits is accomplished over a number of years and constitutes an important part of one's value system. These attributes are not something one brings to the office and then discards on weekends. As a person's career progresses, a track record is continually being molded, and by the time an individual is ready to assume a superintendency, his/her record has become quite well known in the profession. A single major faux pas in any of these areas can do major damage to a reputation that has taken years to build.

A board wants an individual who is able to keep one's ego under control. An ego running wild can create an individual who must always *win*. Every confrontation becomes personal and very competitive in nature. Winning becomes the primary goal as opposed to a resolution that is in the best interests of the students and school system. An overly egotistical individual cannot admit errors in judgment. The personal pronouns *I* and *my* are much used. The superintendent by her/his own admission is the root of all good things that occur within the school system, and s/he begins to refer to the employees as her/his employees and the school district as her/his district.

Superintendents can easily fall into the ego trap. Constantly being the center of attention can be heady business. Before long, instead of just taking the job seriously, the individual is taking himself/herself seriously also. Beware of the lurking ego trap, for superintendents who get caught in its web tend to disappear due to terminal pomposity.

A board wants a superintendent who will be the chief executive officer in fact as well as name. This means being strong in a crisis. It means keeping one's cool when others are losing theirs. It means resolving conflicts in a positive and constructive manner. It means a person who is positive and optimistic. One could go on with other examples. Suffice it to say that being the chief executive officer in fact as well as name means rising above the crowd and assuming a dynamic and positive leadership role.

Last but not least, a board wants a communicator. The board members especially want someone who will communicate with them, promote a positive image of the district, interpret the needs of the district to the public, and maintain positive relationships with the media. This important area is expanded upon in the chapter on the superintendent as communicator.

### Roles and Relationships with the Board

The superintendent must work openly and cooperatively with the board in delineating the roles and responsibilities of each. The traditional policy/administration dichotomy provides a good starting point; however, in practice, this dichotomy is present only in the most general sense.

### *Mission statement development*

The superintendent must work with the board as well as with the other participants in the educational process in developing a mission statement for the system that is acceptable to the board. This is a very important and difficult task for the superintendent because a mission statement that only the superintendent and board believe in will not get the job done. Thus, the superintendent is a catalyst, broker, and negotiator who provides general leadership and oversight in the development of a mission statement acceptable throughout the system.

## Policy development

Once a mission statement has been adopted, the superintendent must help the board develop general policy statements that will give the superintendent guidance in its implementation. During this whole process, the superintendent and board must work as a team with the usual give-and-take, which takes place on an effective policy-setting team. When the team concept, or equilibrium factor, gets out of balance one way or the other, the board/superintendent relationship is in trouble. While some superintendents let their boards struggle by giving them very little guidance, a greater tendency is for the superintendent to assume too much of the board's responsibility. Appropriate board/superintendent equilibrium is very delicate and must be constantly discussed and monitored.

The reality of the superintendent/school board relationship is that both exert leadership and control in performing their respective roles. Leadership and control are not the domain of either party exclusively but rather are situation specific. That is, more often than not, the party exercising leadership and control is determined by the situation that is being addressed and the manner in which it is being addressed. Therefore, the key is not to designate leaders and followers on a permanent basis, but rather to reach agreement on who has the primary responsibility for carrying the ball in a given situation. Moreover, in resolving a complex issue, the ball carrier may change several times during the resolution process.

## Informed board members

Board members want to be kept informed. If something of significance has occurred within the system they need to hear about it from the superintendent first, not from one of their constituents or via a phone call from a reporter or, in the worst case scenario, read about it in the paper or see it on the evening news. In some instances, the superintendent calls each board member personally. In others, a member of the staff calls, or the superintendent calls the board chair who in turn contacts the other board members.

A number of superintendents send a written communication to their board members each week apprising them of recent and upcoming items of interest within the school system. These communiques can often be used to get board members thinking about issues that the superintendent will be bringing before them two or three months down the road.

Board meeting agendas are a very important means of communication with the board. The agenda should be thorough, nicely organized, and accompanied by appropriate supporting material. All board members should be asked for items they wish to have included on the agenda, and in most instances, the superintendent and board chair will cooperatively develop the agenda. The entire packet (agenda and supporting materials) should be delivered to the board members with enough lead time prior to the board meeting so that they will have adequate time to study the materials and contact the superintendent if they have any concerns or questions. Board members should be informed of anything that will be discussed at the meeting. They should never be surprised by the superintendent. Likewise, the superintendent should never be surprised by the board.

On occasion, an individual board member will call the superintendent to inquire about a situation that has come to his/her attention or to request information of some nature. In these instances, the superintendent obviously should be as cooperative and helpful as possible. However, the job may not be complete when the inquiring board member has been satisfied. It is important that all board members have access to the same information and that they all be treated as equals. Thus, it very well may be necessary to inform the other board members of the information provided to one or several board members.

### Implementing and supporting board policies

The superintendent is expected to enthusiastically implement and support board-adopted policies in an equitable manner. This goes even for those policies in which the superintendent may not be in total agreement. In doing this, one may, on occasion, have to protect, defend, and/or speak up on behalf of the board. Under no circumstances should the superintendent indicate that something is being done only because the board asked or mandated that it be done. At times, the superintendent must stoically take some *heat* over board policies. Openly disagreeing with them is not an option. If the superintendent cannot ethically or educationally support a policy or directive of the board and is not able to work with the board to arrive at a mutually acceptable resolution, then resignation is the appropriate alternative.

### Collective bargaining participation

Collective bargaining is a very important part of the superintendent/board relationship. The board, with input and leadership from the superintendent, must determine its bargaining priorities. The board must give guidance to its negotiating team by making decisions on such things as where can compromises be made? What are the top figures for increases in salaries and fringe benefits? What items are worth taking a strike over? etc. The superintendent, in addition to providing accurate information to the board on these matters, must also take a leadership role in keeping things in perspective. For instance, it sometimes is easy for a board member to sit in executive session and indicate that "they can walk before we'll give in on that one." In a situation like this, the superintendent must make sure that the board member(s) really understand all the ramifications of a strike.

It is important that the superintendent as the leader of the board's negotiating team be given some latitude in making decisions at the table. However, it is equally important that the board be kept continuously informed of the progress in negotiations. They need to know what the priorities of the union are, items where agreement has been reached, items that are proving troublesome, etc. They must have a *feel* of how negotiations are proceeding. As the give-and-take of negotiations continues over a period of time, it may be necessary for the superintendent to recommend that the board reconsider some of its previously established negotiating priorities. It will be easier for the board members to understand and accept such a recommendation from the superintendent if they have a sense of the negotiating dynamics that have transpired.

### Budget development

The board should be allowed and encouraged to actively participate in budget development. The budget document is the vehicle by which the board's priorities are funded; it speaks to what the board really believes is important. The board should be given help by the superintendent in understanding the importance of the budgeting process and the implications that budgetary decisions have for the school system. Once the budget has been adopted by the board, the superintendent should be allowed to administer it as long as s/he operates within accepted legal and ethical parameters. The board should be kept apprised of expenditures and encumbrances through appropriate monthly reports and explanations.

### Responding to board requests

On occasion, the board will direct the superintendent to do something on its behalf. As long as the request is not illegal or immoral, the superintendent is expected to do as any good employee would do, which is to carry out the board's directive to the best of one's abilities. Hopefully, the number of board directives issued without reaching prior agreement with the superintendent will be limited to a few. However, there will be some. If the superintendent feels the directive is inappropriate, s/he can fulfill the request and then possibly use it as a springboard for entering into a dialogue with the board so that it does not recur in the future. A superintendent cannot make a big issue out of every infringement on the administrative domain, as the board should not do so each time the superintendent infringes on its domain. There are tolerable limits that both the board and superintendent must constantly strive to stay within.

Requests for special or additional information by the board should be attended to by the superintendent in a timely and thorough fashion. The same advice is true of information requested by an individual board member. However, if an individual board member is constantly requesting information or if several board members make personal requests in an uncoordinated fashion, it may be necessary to discuss the situation with the board chair or the entire board. Sometimes agreement can be reached where individual board member requests will be channeled to the superintendent through the board chair. This will serve to better utilize valuable staff time and will help ensure that all board members are treated equally.

### Respecting privileged communication

The superintendent should respect the confidentiality of privileged conversation with the board and individual board members. This is crucial to maintaining their trust and confidence. However, a word of caution is in order. Entering into privileged communication with individual board members has the potential to silence the superintendent on matters that should be shared with the board. It is also possible that when things shared in confidence become public, as they are prone to do, the superintendent may be accused of withholding important information.

### *Respect for board members*

Board members have a right to be treated with respect. They are the representatives of the community. Sometimes it is difficult to follow this advice when one is being berated by a board member in something less than a respectful manner. However, reciprocating in kind only brings the superintendent down to the level of the berating board member. Two wrongs don't make a right.

### *New board member orientation*

One of the toughest aspects of the superintendency is dealing with the constant turnover of board members. It usually takes about two years for a board member to obtain sufficient knowledge and appreciation of board member roles and responsibilities to be an exemplary board member. Thus, it is very important that the superintendent provide orientation programs for new board members. Many board members have campaigned and got elected as special interest advocates, perhaps to fire the superintendent. Often they have had no prior experience in providing leadership to a large complex organization. Once elected, they can easily become overwhelmed by the situation. They also realize for the first time that an individual board member has no legal authority to hire or fire anyone. The superintendent must help the new board members to function effectively during this on-the-job learning period.

### *Board member constituencies*

Last but not least, the superintendent must realize that every board member, whether elected or appointed, has a constituency. There is a human tendency for people with a perceived problem to want to go straight to the top to get it resolved. Thus, board members will constantly hear complaints, concerns, gossip, rumor, and even a little factual information about the school system. A good board member will learn to use discretion in handling the concerns of individuals. S/he will not find it necessary to share everything with the superintendent.

A new board member will learn, probably the hard way, that there is usually more to a complaint than is initially presented. S/he will learn not to jump to conclusions and make promises based on incomplete and perhaps inaccurate information. It is during this learning process that the superintendent must be understanding but firm in dealing with board member pressures. If a board member(s) is/are responding inappropriately, or perhaps is/are even encouraging inappropriate comments, such as from staff members, the superintendent should professionally address the situation with the board member(s) in a manner that allows the individual(s) to save face. The board chair should be kept informed of such problems.

## Providing Leadership to the School Organization

This portion of the chapter addresses the expectations the board has of the superintendent in implementing its policies within the school system. It does not address how the policies should be implemented because this aspect is addressed in other chapters.

The superintendent is expected to be a child advocate. Other staff members will have vested interests, and often the board will be preoccupied with financial, business, or personnel concerns. It is the responsibility of the superintendent to keep the students on the front burner.

A strong instructional program is expected. Boards tend to rely heavily on superintendents in this area, because instruction usually is the area in which they feel least competent. Instructional items should be a prominent part of each regular board meeting. Board members need to know and be able to explain to others the good educational things that are taking place in the school district.

A fiscally sound operation is a sine qua non. Inappropriate expenditures, even of a minor nature, can quickly discredit the school district and superintendent.

A strong personnel evaluation system should be in place. Accountability is here to stay. With respect to personnel evaluation, the board should have a formal procedure whereby the superintendent is evaluated at least annually. A mid-year progress assessment is gaining popularity.

Strong and supportable decision making is crucial. The superintendent is expected to be open and objective in the decision-making process. S/he is expected to consult appropriate specialists, i.e., lawyers, psychologists, state department of education personnel, etc. in garnering information, and the rationale for such decisions should be thoroughly explained to the board.

It is expected that conflict will be handled in a positive manner. The overall objective is to motivate employees to work toward the achievement of organizational objectives. Conflict resolution and motivation are difficult under the best of circumstances. In a collective bargaining environment, they become even more difficult. Sometimes board members have difficulty in understanding that the superintendent does not directly control a number of activities within the system. At times, the superintendent may be asked to do more than s/he can deliver. Open and continuous communication with the board is necessary to alleviate this type of expectation.

## WORKING WITH THE BOARD OF EDUCATION

### General

### *The board as a filter*

A filter of any type, by definition, serves as a separator. It lets through only that which satisfies predetermined criteria; that which does not satisfy the appropriate criteria is withheld. Depending on the nature of what is being filtered, much or very little original input may make it through the filter.

Each individual has a filter, an immediate boss or a board of directors, through which one's ideas have to be processed. In the case of the superintendent, the board of education serves as the filter. All of the great thoughts, perspectives, imperatives, and recommendations that a superintendent may have go absolutely nowhere if they aren't processed and accepted by the school board.

Every recommendation presented by the superintendent to the board for filtering must have a dividend for the filterers, the board members. Seldom is a board member interested in something that reflects well only on the owner, the superintendent. If the filtering process is not working properly with respect to a particular recommendation, the recommendation probably should be withdrawn and repackaged by the superintendent so that there is a better match between the package and the filtering criteria established by the board.

If a superintendent views the board of education as a filter, the questions and concerns board members have with respect to a particular recommendation can be kept in better perspective. It is more incumbent upon the superintendent to find the right filtering combination than it is upon the board to suspend its filtering process for the benefit of the superintendent.

### Understanding the splinter

There is an adage that if you don't understand the splinter, you won't understand the tree. A superintendent has to read signals very clearly with respect to the school board, administrators, teachers, and citizens. While going around like an Indian scout with one's ear to the ground, it is important to remember that others are doing the same thing. You, in turn, are being read. The processes are reciprocal.

In the superintendency, one must search for and understand the *implication* of everything. Nothing is insignificant that comes to the superintendent. Even the errant and anonymous postcards received complaining about the lousy bus schedule can be splinters. One can gain infections from splinters if they are not given proper attention and removed if at all possible. Constantly striving to be aware of the thoughts and feelings of many publics is a very draining type of commitment that the superintendent accepts; however, this commitment is essential for the well-being of the school system and the survival of the superintendent. Nothing is too insignificant to be given attention. Each splinter constitutes a part of the network of a tree, and if the splinter is ignored, one may be felled by the tree.

### Knowing the board members

There is a need to have both an extensive and an intensive knowledge of the likes, dislikes, and motivations of each board member. It is necessary to know something about the age, employment, economic status, children, grandchildren, vacation plans, clothing likes, hobbies, etc. of each one. All of this information goes together to help the superintendent understand why they vote as they do.

Many times the superintendent is positioned with people who don't particularly care for his/her stance on a given matter. The superintendent is placed in the situation of facing an antagonist on the board who often opposes that which the superintendent is proposing. At this point, the superintendent has to search for reasons. What does the board member have in mind in opposing something that you as the superintendent believe is in the best interest of the children? You know s/he likes children as well as you like children—why is s/he doing this? In an attempt to answer these questions, the superintendent calls up the mental log on the board member and begins to sift through it for answers. What does the board member like, dislike, eat, not eat? Is his/her job in danger? Is s/he in good health? Is his/her spouse and/or mother all right? Is s/he grandstanding for the paper? Is s/he grandstanding for the other board members? Have you as superintendent done something to irritate her/him? Is this retribution or retaliation? What does this all mean? This litany of mental interrogations may take a tenth of a second but often will provide clues to the board member's motivation.

The sooner the superintendent can define the reason for the board member's reaction, the better off s/he will be. In order to do this in a public meeting, it is essential that the superintendent have a wealth of information in mental storage. In essence, it is necessary to keep a *mental book* on each board member. Indeed, each board member is doing the same on the superintendent. Again, the process is reciprocal.

### Changes in superintendent/board relations

The state and national school board associations are telling school board members to do their own homework and to protect themselves from various and sundry liabilities that may arise. Board members are elected by the public and have a constituency to serve. Sometimes the decisions of the superintendent and staff are not politically appealing ones. For these reasons, and probably a host of others, board members are much more questioning today. They are less apt to accept a superintendent's recommendation at face value. They are asking: How do you know that? Where did you gain that impression? What is your source of data? How did you reach that conclusion?

As a result of the extensive questioning received from board members, it is no longer enough for superintendents to just make a recommendation. They must communicate the steps, reference sources, and individuals involved in deriving the recommendation. This is a very time-consuming process, but an essential one in light of the increased interest in the rationale behind recommendations.

Everybody wants to ask the *hard question* that makes the superintendent bleed, or at least sweat heavily. If the superintendent can show that, in addition to his/her questioning, the assistant superintendent, an attorney, several parents, children, and other knowledgeable persons are also being questioned, the superintendent's view becomes much more persuasive. The superintendent's opinion alone is no longer looked upon as superior to the opinions of others.

The superintendent and staff are no longer automatically supported by board members out in the community. Instead, board members are quicker to say let's sit down and talk about it. As a result, the superintendent receives a call from a board member wanting to know if s/he can bring a parent(s) in to talk about a problem. To inform the board member that the parent has bypassed several steps in the resolution process is no longer acceptable. The result is that a meeting is held with the superintendent, appropriate staff, the parent(s), and board member in attendance. The board member tends to be an observer during the meeting, a sort of informal arbiter, making mental notes about how adequately the superintendent and staff support their decision. If the superintendent is able to make a case for a well-researched and reasoned decision, the board member probably will be less quick to request such meetings in the future. However, most board members have to go through this trial by fire before they become convinced that the superintendent's decisions are worthy of their support.

The superintendent's decisions, more and more, are refined judgments based on information gleaned from a number of sources. The superintendent must become an astute consultor of specialists. This role has become so important that a subsequent chapter has been devoted to it exclusively.

## Relationships with the Board as an Entity

### Communicating with the board

The manner in which a superintendent communicates with the board varies with the size of the district and the leadership style of the superintendent. Some superintendents communicate weekly in writing while others communicate daily and have all messages hand delivered. However, there are some general guidelines that prove helpful.

It is preferable to have information provided to board members by the superintendent and staff rather than by the media, angry parents, or some group calling them. In providing information to board members, always let them know whom to contact if they wish to pursue it further. Often their choice will be to call the superintendent, but this does not have to be the case. Depending on the size and competence of the superintendent's staff, individuals other than the superintendent can be listed as the contact persons. This conserves the valuable time of the superintendent, gives the appearance of a competent administrative team, and gives board members options for obtaining their information.

For the team concept to work in responding to board members, the superintendent must have a great deal of confidence in both himself/herself and the staff. There must not be a feeling that somebody is going to upstage somebody else. A trust level must exist that has been earned through a number of experiences. The team approach also implies that any one of several individuals can respond on behalf of the superintendent to important system concerns. This does not just happen. It takes a considerable amount of meeting time daily to arrive at common understandings and approaches.

In summary, communicating with the board is a time-consuming and terribly important process, and thus, a team approach is suggested.

### Superintendent expectations of the board

Probably the greatest expectation a superintendent should have of the board is that they let him/her speak. A superintendent should have the opportunity to express his/her thinking, feelings, and perceptions. S/he should not filibuster but should have the opportunity to speak uninterruptedly about the rationale for a recommendation. Given this opportunity, the board should then have the opportunity to question the superintendent.

It is important for the superintendent to keep in mind that the board many times does not understand where s/he is going or why. What the board members understand on one given day in terms of organizational direction may become hazy in three days. The superintendent has to constantly reestablish his/her bearings with the board. They must be given a directional reading frequently.

## *Board member orientation*

There is general agreement that not enough work is done in this area at the local level. State associations have a number of meetings on boardsmanship and good publications are available on a host of topics. These are all very important; however, the highest priority for board member orientation at the local level is to establish a feeling of openness with and access to the superintendent and administrative staff. There are many ways this can be done. One successful method is to establish an open lunch period several days a week at which time any board member knows that s/he can stop in and see the superintendent and/or members of his/her staff. If a board member cannot come in at this time, s/he knows the superintendent and staff are available for phone calls. The same concept can be used on Saturday mornings. Whatever the strategy, it is imperative that the board members come to believe in all sincerity that the superintendent and his/her staff are available to discuss any topic of interest to them.

Involving board members in committee work with staff members is a good way for board members to gain expertise and to establish a personal working relationship with staff. Standing committees can include such things as facilities, finances, employed personnel, student personnel, legislation, etc. Ad hoc committees can be used effectively to study such items as discipline policies and grading policies, etc. These committees should be established for a specific purpose and for a specified period of time.

An offshoot of the committee approach is to have specific staff members develop special relationships with individual board members. These relationships can be very positive factors in the communication process. Again, trusting relationships must exist between the superintendent and staff for this approach to work effectively.

## *Importance of secretaries*

A capable superintendent's secretary is almost an assistant superintendent in terms of what s/he knows about school operations and how s/he interacts with people. This individual has to be proficient in the usual secretarial types of tasks; however, the most important attribute is that s/he know how to work with the public. Often a board member would rather talk initially with the secretary than with the superintendent. S/he may feel more comfortable in conveying a request to the secretary or in venting dissatisfaction. The secretary can channel a request to the appropriate staff member or help calm down an irate individual both of which can save damaged feelings and enhance communication between the superintendent and board.

The same trust should exist between a superintendent and his/her secretary that exists with the professional staff. If the secretary is to function effectively, s/he must be as fully informed as any professional staff member.

## Superintendent evaluation by the board

Superintendents are usually evaluated formally once a year. If the formal evaluation process is working properly, mutually agreed upon goals and objectives for the superintendent and school system will be established, and the evaluation will focus on the degree to which the goals and objectives have been met. These goals and objectives can be used as guides for personal time allocation and for time allocation at board meetings. How do individual acts by the superintendent and board further one or more of the goals or objectives should be a constantly asked question.

The reality of the evaluation situation is that it is never quite as clear and concise as that depicted. Instead, the superintendent is being evaluated daily by board members. Every time a board member reads the paper or talks with a constituent, some type of impression is being made. Every time the superintendent makes a presentation to a senior citizens' group, to the board of realtors, to the Chamber of Commerce, etc., s/he is being evaluated. Every time a board member sends a note or makes a call, the superintendent is being evaluated. Perceptions developed informally in these ways by board members will be reflected in the formal evaluation.

The tenor of board meetings can be an indicator of the informal evaluations being formed by board members. Recommendations that are constantly running into trouble, public and private expressions of concern about the school system, or comments such as "I thought we put that one to rest six months ago" are revealing with respect to informal board member evaluations. An alert and perceptive superintendent who is attuned to the nuances of the informal evaluation process should never be surprised by the contents of the formal evaluation.

## Relationships with Individual Board Members

### *Communicating with individual board members*

The desire to respond to the concerns of individual board members and at the same time not provide individual board members with privileged information is a dilemma faced by superintendents. An approach to this dilemma that usually works is as follows. When an individual board member calls to request information relative to a particular concern, ask the board member if s/he cares if you share the concern with the other board members and staff. Usually there will be a pause, and then the board member response will be "yes, you probably should." At this point, involve appropriate staff members in collecting data and formulating a response.

Always put the response in writing. In addition to stating the specific concern and the formulated response to the concern, also (1) indicate that the letter will be shared with the other board members (2) name the staff members who were involved in formulating the response (3) indicate the number of staff hours required to formulate the response and (4) indicate that if the response is incomplete, any of the board members should feel free to contact the superintendent or any of the listed staff.

### *Board member infringement upon superintendent prerogatives*

A board member becoming overly concerned and involved with employment practices or the general day-to-day operation of the schools is at one time or another a problem for every superintendent. If the superintendent disagrees with the action of a board member, s/he has to find a way to let the board member know that s/he is uncomfortable with the situation. A good first approach usually is to let the board member know that you respect what s/he has to say, but that s/he is only one-fifth or one-seventh of the board, and that her/his concerns should be brought before the entire board for their consideration. Beware of deal making with individual board members. This type of action has resurfaced to haunt many a superintendent.

If the board member persists at a board meeting, the superintendent should request the opportunity to respond without interruption to the issue. The superintendent's response may not dissuade the dissident board member, but other board members expect the superintendent to rise to the occasion and respond logically to his/her criticism. Thus, on occasion the superintendent will have to stand up and be counted, in an unpopular situation where feelings can get bruised. But to do otherwise means that you allow yourself and/or your staff to be (1) subverted, (2) intimidated, or (3) completely neutralized when you are being paid to be a leader.

In dealing with a problem board member, the telephone sometimes is not the best means to resolve a disagreement. Although much communication takes place on the telephone, however, it usually is not a good instrument of persuasion. In a problem situation, there is more credence in open discussion where everyone has a chance to speak and to listen. In this forum, reconciliation is apt to come from another board member. Or, another board member can provide a cooling affect by saying, "Hey, this conversation has degenerated. Let's see if we can't find a resolution." If another board member has a good suggestion, don't hesitate to recognize the suggestion as such. This places the dissident board member in the position of going along or being isolated.

Of course, informal and amicable means for working out disagreements represent the preferred route; however, there will be times when this is not possible. The superintendent needs to make plans for handling these situations.

### Board member criticism of the superintendent in the media

One should go to great lengths to avoid a debate through the media. After a board member unloads on the superintendent via the media, the superintendent should first search his/her mental file in an attempt to ascertain the real reasons for the outburst. Trusted staff can also be very valuable in this effort. Second, if the superintendent is contacted by the media for a response, s/he should state the rationale for the decision or position but not criticize the board member. Third, contact the board member and let him/her know that this type of behavior benefits neither of you, and that perhaps the two of you should have a debate at an open board meeting. Usually the board member will respond that his/her real intent was not conveyed by the reporter. Sometimes this can be used as an entree for a discussion on how items can be handled differently in the future.

If a board member persists with media criticisms, s/he should be again reminded that s/he is only one-fifth or one-seventh of the board and will be looked upon as such. At this point, it is important to get a good reading of the other board members. As discussed earlier, one must make sure that what one thinks is a splinter is not in reality a branch, a trunk, or a whole tree. Nothing should be taken lightly. Avoid at all costs a confederation of board members aligned against something the superintendent is doing because ultimately, the superintendent will lose. Other board members often are the most influential in bringing a recalcitrant board member back into the fold.

### Facility visitation by board members

Most board members visit facilities upon invitation. Usually the superintendent will receive an invitation also. When this is the case, the superintendent or a member of the staff should make a concerted effort to be in attendance.

If a board member drops in unannounced at a facility, the principal should be prepared to take things in stride. S/he should inform the superintendent of the visit. This is particularly true in smaller systems or if the board member has raised some questions, questioned the cleanliness of the building, or in other ways has expressed dissatisfaction about a particular facility. Unannounced visits tend to be more common today than in years past.

### Socializing with board members

There are varying opinions with respect to socializing with board members. However, a good rule of thumb is to keep the superintendent/board member relationship pure and professional. Socializing with individual board members and their spouses tends to distract from the overall picture. The spouses may not get along or may say something that is questionable, at least. In addition, there is always the possibility that perceptions will emerge within the community that a particular board member(s) is in the hip pocket of the superintendent or vice versa. Neither perception is desirable.

Of course, there will be social occasions where the entire board, the superintendent, and spouses will be in attendance. This is a part of the superintendency and a part in which the superintendent's spouse plays a vital role.

## Board Meetings

### *Agenda*

The superintendent usually takes the lead in putting together an agenda for a board meeting. Often the board chair is consulted prior to finalizing the agenda. If the board meeting is on Monday, the agenda should be in place by Wednesday of the preceding week and hand delivered to the board members on Thursday. This gives them a chance to review the materials and, if need be, ask for clarification or suggest additional item(s) for the agenda.

Many formats are available for organizing the board agenda and its supporting materials. Whatever the format, the agenda should have a logical organization, be clear and concise, and be cross-referenced with supporting material.

There are differing opinions as to how much supporting material should be provided with the agenda. Some superintendents feel that too much supporting material tends to overwhelm board members to the point where they either do not read the material or else become confused by it. However, the prevailing feeling is that it is better to err on the side of providing too much information. If a board member does not study all of the material at one time, s/he should be encouraged to develop a filing system so that reference may be made to any number of topics throughout the year. Some superintendents help their board establish a personal filing system for the benefit of consistency. When this is done, supporting material should be coded as to its file.

### *Procedures*

Many board meetings are held in the evening; however, there is a trend to schedule more meetings in the late afternoon. Afternoon meetings have been criticized for being at a time of day that limits citizen participation, but attendance figures at board meetings do not seem to support this. People make the meeting regardless of the time. For some unknown reason, evening meetings tend to lend themselves to more distractions and deviations.

There is merit to holding executive sessions prior to the regular board meeting. This establishes an ending time for the session, and sensitive items will be discussed before fatigue sets in. An added benefit is that the regular meeting runs in a more orderly fashion with less sensationalism once the tension has been released in the executive session.

In addition to following Robert's Rules of Order, there should be guidelines as to how additional items may be added to the agenda. Some boards are very strict, allowing no new items to be added to the agenda during the meeting. Others take a more lenient approach and will address concerns from the audience at the end of a meeting. If there isn't time, the item is placed first on the next meeting's agenda. It is important to note that discussing a concern does not mean that action has to be taken on it. In fact, in most instances, it would not be wise to do so without time for reflection.

As a rule, most boards and superintendents try to establish a policy of *no surprises*. If and when the superintendent does get surprised at a meeting, action should be postponed if at all possible. Hasty and poorly researched judgments make for bad decisions.

Seating arrangements at board meetings are a personal preference. However, a case can be made that the superintendent should sit next to the board chairperson because they may be communicating throughout the meeting. A word of caution is in order. The superintendent must take precautions to ensure that the board and audience perceive that the board chairperson is actually in control of the meeting. Seats on coasters make it easier for the superintendent to unobtrusively confer with staff or other board members during the meeting.

### Citizen participation

Every board should have a policy and guidelines addressing citizen participation. Most guidelines require the individual wishing to address the board to submit his/her name and topic to the board office at a specified time prior to the board meeting. If a group with a common interest will be in attendance, the group is asked to designate a spokesperson. Often a time limit per speaker of three to five minutes is established.

Boards often are reluctant to limit the number of presenters or curb the length of presentations. It is at these times that the superintendent, in conjunction with the board chairperson, must intervene. If the issue is a contested one, the superintendent or board chair may say, "We have heard three pros and three cons. I think we understand the issue. We will study the issue and formulate a written response." The worst way to handle the situation is to ask, "Does anyone else wish to address the board?" Following this question, individuals who had no intention of addressing the board will be moved to try their hand on center stage.

Sometimes an individual will be permitted to address the board with a concern directly related to school operations. In such a situation, the superintendent should resist the urge to chastise the individual for not giving the staff a chance to work on the problem. The superintendent should take matters as they are and proceed from that point.

If citizens wish to address the Board with a common concern, the board, after hearing representative concerns, should attempt to have these individuals meet with the superintendent or staff member. In this way, the staff will work with the group.

In recent years, there has been a tendency for more and more individuals to address the board. The media loves this action. It is much more exciting than the purchase of textbooks, toilet tissue, and supplies. At times, the media will blow a rather mundane circumstance out of proportion.

Citizen participation at board meetings is another sliver that should not be ignored. Once their concerns have been made public, some type of response from the superintendent's office is required. Often, much staff time is necessary to adequately respond to these concerns.

### Leadership role for the superintendent

In addition to presenting the recommendations and giving background information, the superintendent must rise to the occasion as critical situations emerge during board meetings. As Jack Kennedy said, "It is amazing what one person can do in a critical moment to turn things around." That one person could be the superintendent.

Board members should be recognized by the public as independent thinkers. They do perform yeoman duty and deserve credit for their civic contributions; however, in moments of crisis during board meetings, they usually turn to the superintendent to carry the ball. There is the expectation that the superintendent should put the figurative noose around his/her neck and then adroitly work his/her way out of it. Every superintendent worth his salt must noose himself/herself occasionally. This is part of being a real leader.

## CONCLUDING COMMENT

The superintendent/school board relationship is the leadership keystone for the school system. Thus, it is appropriate that this discussion constitutes the longest chapter in this book.

# CHAPTER 13

# The Superintendent as Negotiator

In the current era, there is probably nothing that has a greater impact on the day-to-day operation of a school system and staff morale within the system than the collective bargaining process and the formal collective bargaining agreement. In some states, the collective bargaining agreement is so prominent that its contents take precedence over state law. It is obvious that a process and document that collectively exert such a great influence on a school district must be of primary concern to the superintendent.

It is imperative that a superintendent give careful thought to the role s/he can best serve in the collective bargaining process. The purpose of this chapter is to explore the pros and cons of the two primary roles the superintendent can play in the collective bargaining process. The superintendent will be either the chief negotiator for the board or s/he will serve in a coordinating and data-gathering capacity while an individual employed from outside the system serves as the board's spokesperson. There is no *right* answer to this dilemma. It is situation and individual specific.

The chapter begins by identifying some differences between public sector and private sector bargaining. The second section presents a

Mr. Leigh Herington, Esq. furnished the basic material for the first two sections. Mr. Herington is an attorney who is employed by numerous boards of education to serve as their spokesperson. Mr. Herington also has served as chair of a board of education.

Dr. Norman Sommers furnished the basic material for the third section. Dr. Sommers has been superintendent of the Cardinal Local Schools in Ohio for twenty years. He has served as the chief spokesperson for the board during the entire twenty years. He also conducts workshops and has published articles relative to the superintendent as spokesperson.

case for employing an outside negotiator. This section also discusses the role of the superintendent when someone else is serving as the chief spokesperson. The third section presents a case for the superintendent serving as the board's chief spokesperson. This section concludes with some negotiating suggestions for the superintendent.

## PUBLIC SCHOOL VS. PRIVATE SECTOR BARGAINING

When negotiations take place between a labor union and a for-profit company, the results are different than when they take place between a labor union and a publicly funded organization. In the private sector, by keeping a dollar away from the employees, a dollar has been saved for stockholders. In the public school context, the result is a delicate balance between prudent expenditure of public funds and appropriate wages for school employees. Determining a prudent expenditure of public funds for school employee salaries is a difficult dilemma. Generally, communities have a desire to pay their teachers well; however, individual community members also have a desire to pay as little in taxes as possible.

Public school negotiations actually become a negotiation with the community as well as the school staff. The job of the board's negotiating team is to determine an appropriate salary and benefit package that is within the confines of what the community is willing to accept. The correct determination of this package will have a significant bearing on whether the community will support the schools in the future, as well as being instrumental in determining future relationships between the school staff, administration, and board of education.

The achievement of the correct balance for the salary and fringe benefit package can also have a lot to do with how good the school district feels about itself. Teachers tend to be more productive when they perceive that they are paid appropriately and that they work in a community that appreciates its school system.

The other critical difference in public school negotiations is the potential for various nonmonetary issues to cripple the administration's ability to promote and require good education and good teaching within the school system. Things like just cause for nonrenewal, limitations on teacher transfers, restrictions on reductions-in-force, restrictive evaluation procedures, etc. can negatively curtail the ability of a school district to provide quality education.

## HIRED GUN AS SPOKESPERSON

### Why Hire an Outside Gun as Spokesperson?

There are six reasons for employing an individual from outside the school system to serve as the chief spokesperson for the board. Each reason is presented and discussed below.

### An understanding of and feel for the process

Negotiations is a dynamic and strategic process. The art of negotiations is one in which there are no specific ground rules or guidelines. This is unlike a court of law in which there are established rules of evidence and procedure. Although techniques are important in negotiations, there are no rules that are required to be followed when two parties meet at the negotiating table.

Often the negotiations context and the dynamics of the process are much more important than the subject matter of the negotiations. For this reason, whoever is responsible for the coordination of the negotiations for the board must be responsible for a vision of the entire process. This vision must start with the perceived end result and move backward to the initial contact. The strategies involved in the development of this process are very important. A professional negotiator is more attuned to the nuances of the process and more skilled in developing a strategy that will lead to positive results.

Initial positions need to be handled very carefully. Often presentations and reactions at this stage are as important as any future developments. It may be that the initial contact requires very aggressive behavior from the management team. On the other hand, certain circumstances require a cooperative approach. Strategy for the initial presentation and reaction to proposals are difficult points in the process. A professional negotiator can be very helpful in the decision-making process during this aspect of the negotiations.

An important dynamic of negotiations is that the parties begin to build bridges through the process so that a feeling of mutual trust and respect can evolve. The development of this type of climate often is identified as the reason for a successful negotiating process. Developing this climate in a confrontational environment takes a special skill that is developed by participating in the negotiations process on a continuing basis.

### An understanding of contract language

Regardless of whether or not the teachers' association uses a professional negotiator as its spokesperson, the association always receives assistance from professionals in formulating the language used in proposals. The nature of contract language and the board's response are important. Unless the board's team has a full understanding of language implications, they could inadvertently agree to problematic language that appears harmless but is actually very harmful. For instance, if the board agrees to language that was presented by the staff but was actually developed by the union professionals, at some later date the union could bring in its professionals in a language dispute to give their interpretations of the intent of the language. Because they (the union) wrote the language, their testimony would be persuasive.

Also, it is important to have knowledge on how contract language will be interpreted by a court of law, an arbitrator, or a third-party neutral.

A board negotiating team that is led by an in-house spokesperson often is very reluctant, as it should be, to enter into signed agreements on language that has been recommended by the teachers' association. As a result, negotiations can be delayed for as much as a month or more because of the insecurity and reluctance on the part of the board's team to reach agreement on language.

In contrast, a professional negotiator is expected to immediately understand the significance of the language and to advise management on any language-related problems. A professional negotiator should also be able to present counterproposals in appropriate language without unnecessary delay. An ability to quickly analyze language and respond appropriately can be a big asset in bringing negotiations to a productive conclusion.

Very few negotiations are completed without some self-imposed deadlines that result in *zero hour* marathon bargaining sessions. Under these conditions, analysis and immediate response abilities are invaluable. The professional negotiator earns his/her keep under such conditions. A good professional negotiator can assure that last minute decisions and language agreements do not contain undetected hidden costs and/or problematic language.

### *An ability to separate the wheat from the chaff*

The individuals in charge of the negotiations need to have the ability to understand what is important, when it is important to settle certain issues, and when to stand firm on others. Early negotiation strategies and settlement of minor issues become very important to the overall progress of negotiations. The more time that is spent on an item, the more important it becomes. Therefore, it is important not to let a minor item for the board get blown out of proportion. The professional negotiator, in part, is paid for knowing when to resolve certain items and when to resist settlement.

### *Professionals dealing with professionals*

Professional negotiators for the board and the teachers' association constantly come in contact with and negotiate against each other on *the circuit*. Thus, no one particular negotiating session is so important that one party is going to ruin his/her credibility with the other party for future negotiating sessions. Even though each party is forcefully representing the interests of his/her side, over time, a mutual respect and understanding develops between the two negotiators. As a result, there is less of an inclination to take advantage of the individual on the other side or to offer language that a professional will be unlikely to accept. Unreasonable positions are not apt to be held as tenuously as might be the case with an in-house negotiator.

### *Ability to devote an appropriate amount of time to the negotiations process*

Superintendents and other administrators are required to spend extremely long hours providing general leadership to the school district. Negotiating in and of itself is a time-consuming process, often lasting months. To add the role of spokesperson to the superintendent's already overcrowded agenda would present an untenable time commitment. Something would have to give. Either the schools would be lacking in leadership during the negotiating period, or the negotiations process would receive inadequate attention and preparation. Neither alternative is an acceptable one.

### *Preserving the superintendent's relationship with the board*

The importance of the relationship between the superintendent and the board of education is a major reason the majority of superintendents should not attempt to go through the negotiations process without professional assistance. The first obstacle is preparing the board for negotiations. Traditionally, boards begin the negotiations process by being very aggressive. They believe that the board's negotiating team should have very little latitude in the negotiating process. It is important that the board be made to understand that this is not an appropriate attitude. They must understand that negotiations is a dynamic give-and-take process. If there is to be a satisfactory conclusion, compromises must be made along the way. An outside professional negotiator can often be more direct in addressing the board relative to these matters.

As the negotiating process progresses, it is likely there will not be unanimity among the board members on strategy, what concessions must be made, the presentation of final offers, etc. As a result, some will probably be unhappy with decisions reached. If this unhappiness is directed at the superintendent, it could impair relationships long after the contract is settled.

By being actively involved in the negotiating process, but not as the spokesperson, the superintendent avoids much of the unpleasantness at the table that could have long-range implications on his/her staff relations. If the negotiations go well, the superintendent can receive a lion's share of the credit; if they prove troublesome, the hired gun can take the brunt of the criticism.

### The Role of the Superintendent

The most important thing that a superintendent can do for the negotiations process is to continually work toward the development of a positive labor relations climate. How the staff feels at any given time will have a major impact on the problems and language that come to the table. For instance, a contract that has resulted in few grievances and questions of interpretation will mean a smaller new package with fewer changes brought to the table by the union.

The attitude taken by the staff when they come to the table is also affected by the general labor relations climate within the district. The superintendent must be certain that the spokesperson is fully aware of the labor relations dynamics that have transpired in the district since the last negotiations.

With respect to the actual negotiations process, the superintendent as the chief executive officer of the board must always be in control of the process. S/he must advise the spokesperson on such things as the goals of the board, what management would specifically like to see accomplished, and the attitude to be displayed by the board's team during negotiations.

The superintendent must be the leader in the development of the board's proposals and counterproposals. In providing this leadership, s/he must coordinate the thoughts and efforts of the board, other administrators, and the spokesperson. After the proposals have been developed, the superintendent must work with the spokesperson to jointly determine the strategies that will be used in presenting and defending the proposals at the table.

Once negotiations begin at the table, the superintendent should be available at all times, preferably at the table, to monitor progress and to make certain that the board's goals are being met. If there is a variance from the strategies previously developed, the superintendent must work closely with the spokesperson to alter plans appropriately. The superintendent must then inform the board of these changes. In fact, the superintendent must continuously keep the board informed of the progress and dynamics taking place during the negotiations.

It is essential that the superintendent keep the *pipe lines* open during negotiations. He must obtain information via a number of sources relative to the dynamics within the staff, community, and board. The potential pressures exerted by one side on the other are central to the negotiation process. The superintendent must have a good barometer to accurately perceive the ebb and flow of feelings. S/he must share these perceptions with the spokesperson and board.

A key role of the superintendent is to oversee the analysis of financial data and the development of the board's financial proposals and counterproposals. These analyses and proposals must be accurate because they determine the financial parameters within which the board must negotiate. A mistake in either direction can have a negative impact on the district for years to come.

In summary, the superintendent plays a crucial role in the negotiations process, even when a hired gun is used as the spokesperson.

S/he has a major responsibility in helping the board establish viable negotiating goals and s/he also retains responsibility as the ultimate decision maker during the day-to-day negotiating process.

## THE SUPERINTENDENT AS SPOKESPERSON

### Traditional Assumptions

Conventional wisdom in educational administration has dictated against the superintendent serving as the spokesperson for the board during negotiations. This time-honored position has generally been supported by three assumptions. First, the superintendent will somehow destroy her/his ability to provide leadership to the district if s/he becomes involved in the confrontational activities of collective bargaining. Second, it takes a tremendous amount of time and energy to negotiate. This is time and energy taken away from the other important activities of the superintendent. In general, the negotiation process will tend to overshadow all of the other activities. Third, the superintendent is probably not an expert in negotiations. Thus, a skilled outside professional negotiator will do a better job.

Each of these bits of conventional wisdom can be challenged. The dangers of losing educational leadership ability because of confrontation can be challenged on two fronts. The first is that no successful leader has ever led without some confrontation. Being able to lead in the face of, and in spite of, confrontation is a sign of a good leader. The second is that serious confrontation is not necessary in the negotiation process. A good negotiator can reach agreement successfully with a minimum of real confrontation (real as opposed to the usual theatrics inherent in the playing out of roles by the participants in the game).

The second assumption is that the amount of time and energy taken away from other more important activities in a superintendent's life places the negotiation of an acceptable contract much too low on the superintendent's priority list. However, in the contemporary setting, one of the most important things a superintendent can do is negotiate a good contract. All the excellent work done on curriculum, academic achievement, staff relations, community relations, etc. will be for naught if the negotiated contract does not permit the superintendent to effectively lead the school district.

The contract is binding on all who work in the school district. It can be the single most important document in the working life of the staff and management. It sets salary, working conditions, and the parameters within which the staff, administrators, superintendent, and school board will relate to each other. As superintendent, one cannot afford to leave such an important piece of work in the hands of an outsider who will leave as soon as the contract is settled. Also, in all likelihood, the professional negotiator will not be an educator and will not fully comprehend the nuances inherent to an educational organization.

The third statement that the superintendent is not a negotiations expert and does not work at it every day assumes that a superintendent cannot become a good negotiator. In reality, all superintendents negotiate every day. Successful negotiations is an ongoing process that is carried out daily with every contact the members of the management team have with the other employees in the district.

**Advantages Gained by Serving as the Spokesperson**

If a superintendent is to advantageously use the negotiation process as a management tool, then the process must take place year around. The psychological preparation, the planting of ideas, and the analysis of current operations and attitudes must be done daily throughout the year. All of these things have a bearing on what takes place at the negotiating table. They must be used advantageously at the table to achieve optimal contract language. An outside negotiator cannot do this because s/he is not in the system on a daily basis.

Everything that affects the staff affects negotiations. Thus, everything the school board, superintendent, and principals do affects negotiations. These daily activities establish the atmosphere and tone which will prevail at the table.

Another key to successful negotiations is *trust*. This seems so obvious that it need not be mentioned, but unfortunately, it is often not present at the bargaining table. Trust is an elusive element that is somewhat mercurial in nature and has many forces working to drive it away. It takes daily effort over a long period of time to achieve and yet, a single incident by someone unfamiliar with a situation can destroy it immediately.

Trust can be built at the bargaining table. As an example, on one occasion, a union put a proposal on the table asking for less sick leave and lower severance pay than they already had. This was an obvious mix-up, but under the rules at the table it was irretrievable. The choices for the superintendent were clear: accept that part of the proposal as written and get three years of less sick leave and lower severance pay or gently let the union save face. The board's decision to go with a timely rejection of this proposal along with a suggestion that sick leave and severance pay be brought back to the current level achieved two things. First, it prevented bitter feelings and resentment that would have been forthcoming on the part of the union leaders when they realized that the superintendent had embarrassed them by capitalizing on their mistake. Second, it made the superintendent look more competent and caring about the staff members than the union. This did nothing but enhance the positive psychological image of the superintendent with the staff.

The third primary key is the achievement of a *we win* attitude at the conclusion of negotiations. This is not to be confused with the *win-win* process of negotiating. *Win-win* can be used advantageously, but it is a process. *We win* is a state of mind that can be achieved via a variety of mechanical processes. *We win* is essential to successful, nonconfrontational negotiations. One can have things come out the way one wants and still not antagonize the staff. This takes a conscious effort. It involves looking at things from the other person's point of view. It does not mean giving in to all union demands.

*We win* means simply that when the collective bargaining process is over, both sides will feel good about the settlement. There will be few settlements in which both parties are completely satisfied with the agreement, but a feeling and sense of satisfaction must be there for both.

### Self-Assessment

In order to capitalize on the advantages outlined above, the spokesperson for the board must possess the appropriate personal traits and mind-set. A self-assessment of these items is in order to aid one in making the decision to serve as the spokesperson. By both formal and informal means, one needs to obtain answers to the following questions: How do I lead? What is my dominant leadership style? What is my dominant decision-making style? What makes me react? What is my value system? etc. It is important to develop a personal profile of this nature in order to get a handle on how one is likely to react in the role of spokesperson.

The union members will be making judgments of their own relative to the superintendent's personal traits. They will attempt to use these traits to their advantage during negotiations. For example, if the union perceives the superintendent as an impatient person, it may prolong negotiations in the hopes of obtaining more favorable concessions from the superintendent who wants the negotiations to progress at a more rapid pace and is eager to bring closure to the entire process. If it perceives the superintendent as a combative, reactive sort, it will attempt to goad him/her into personal confrontations and rash reactions. If the superintendent has great pride in being fair, the union will couch its demands in terms of fairness, e.g., it is only fair that no teacher should have more than twenty-five students in a class because some teachers have classes with as few as fifteen enrolled. Or, if the superintendent likes to be perceived as a very logical individual, the union may present its class size argument in terms of logic, e.g., smaller classes are bound to enhance the learning environment because there will be fewer disruptions, fewer papers to grade, the students will receive more individualized attention, etc.

If the self-analysis process uncovers some factors that could be detrimental to one's effectiveness as a spokesperson, one must make some decisions relative to the severity with which they will impact on the spokesperson's role. It also is necessary to assess the level of motivation one has to learn and practice new and more appropriate behavior patterns. While there is some debate on the issue, there is evidence that one's behavior patterns can be changed if there is a commitment to do so.

The mind-set one has toward the bargaining process is the second factor that must be addressed when making a decision on serving as the board's spokesperson. If one looks upon collective bargaining as a big game—a big game that makes poor use of valuable time—this attitude will quickly become evident at the table. If one does not feel comfortable entering into personal and intense give-and-take for hours at a time, serving as the spokesperson will be a very trying experience. In fact, if one dreads the thought of bargaining for whatever reasons, the spokesperson's role will not be a positive experience.

It has been said that if one does not envy the role of a trial lawyer, then one probably will not enjoy negotiating. One has to be challenged and get a *high* out of the process. One has to look forward to and enjoy being a participant in the process.

Under no circumstances should one agree to be the chief spokesperson at the table unless one has observed and participated in a contract negotiation in some capacity. There is a feel for the process that is difficult to put into words. Negotiations is a game, a serious one, but a game nonetheless. Like all other games, it has rules, both written and unwritten. The written rules come from collective bargaining law and procedures, and the unwritten rules come from the process, psychology, and strategy. To use an analogy, in poker the written rules say a flush beats a straight and three-of-a-kind beats a pair. An unwritten rule says never draw to an inside straight. Winning poker players have learned both the written and unwritten rules. They know when to raise and when to fold. They know how to read other players. A good spokesperson is like a good poker player.

In the final analysis, if one decides to take on the role of spokesperson, this responsibility will be in addition to the other negotiating responsibilities discussed earlier in the chapter. The superintendent must still be the general overseeing the negotiation process and in addition, now will be serving as the platoon leader.

## The Psychology of Negotiating

Most books on collective negotiations deal with things like the law, labor board rulings, unfair labor practices, arbitration, and language. These are all things in which a negotiator should be well-versed, but the real secret of negotiation success resides in the psychological dimension. As a basis for the discussion on the psychology of negotiations, Maslow's hierarchy of needs and Herzberg's motivation-hygiene theory, as explained in the chapter on motivation, are used.

Much of what is negotiated is at the first two levels of Maslow's hierarchy, the physiological and safety-security levels. Such things as salary, fringe benefits, tenure, fair dismissal, and working conditions fall into these categories. According to Herzberg, satisfaction of needs at this level will keep productivity from decreasing but will not bring about increased productivity.

In reality, the alleged physiological and safety-security factors identified in the preceding paragraph may be symbols for something else. For instance, teachers' salaries are at a point where under ordinary circumstances their basic physiological needs are satisfied. Likewise, the education profession enjoys safety-security provisions like few other professions due to tenure laws and, in a number of states, strong retirement systems. If this is the case, what psychological needs are being fulfilled by the negotiation of these factors? There is some evidence that these things are not only important in and of themselves but also represent a tangible way of comparing oneself with other professionals. In other words, a higher order need, esteem, is involved. How am I valued in relation to my colleagues in other districts?

A good example of this phenomenon is illustrated in the case of two adjacent school districts of similar size and resources who were negotiating at the same time. The teachers in system A had agreed among themselves to settle for a salary increase of 4.5 percent. However, before this amount could be formalized at the table, system B agreed to a 5 percent salary increase. Immediately, the teachers in system A raised their ante to 5.2 percent. The end result was a bitter strike. It is quite clear from this scenario that ego and esteem were much more the issues than the monetary amount.

Physiological and safety-security needs cannot be ignored, for they must be fulfilled before the staff moves up to higher order needs. However, if it can be assumed for the moment that physiological and safety-security needs are being addressed reasonably well in most situations, what about the next higher need level on Maslow's hierarchy, the social need level? It is human nature for people to want to belong to a group(s) that will give them a sense of belonging and identity. This is the reason high school students buy school jackets and class rings. This same approach will work with the staff at very little expense to the board. Such things as staff athletic teams, TGIF parties, picnics, breakfasts, coffee mugs, key rings, caps, tote bags, etc. can be addressed at minimal cost. The superintendent should be ever alert to ways in which loyalty to a school building and/or the school system can be promoted. Individuals who have a strong sense of being a part of the district team or the school family are less likely to have a strong militant bond with the union. Loyalty tends to follow identity. The cost and time involved in promoting a sense of identity away from the table is very minimal when compared to the price that likely will be paid at the table.

The goal of the superintendent should be to fulfill the lower order needs on Maslow's hierarchy so that as much time as possible may be spent at the esteem level. At this level, the individuals value being perceived as competent responsible professionals. Satisfaction of needs at the esteem level falls into Herzberg's motivation category, which means that productivity within the system can be increased by negotiating at this level.

At the esteem level, inclusion in decision-making processes and assumption of responsibilities for outcomes become important items. The information contained in the chapter on empowering is crucial to fulfilling needs at the esteem level.

Esteem needs vary by individual. Thus, more creativity and innovativeness must be used in the negotiation process. However, a simple two-letter word used both at the table and on a daily basis can do wonders in this area. This two-letter word is *we*.

When the superintendent says to the union representative, or whoever the significant other is, "We have a problem. Please help me solve it," the ownership of the problem has been shared. It has become our problem to solve, therefore we must work together to arrive at our solution. The significant other now has partial ownership of the problem as well as a partial ownership of the solution. This approach gives the superintendent the chance to get in some positive strokes. It also provides the opportunity to give the significant others credit at an appropriate time.

It is important not to ruin others' esteem at the table. This means that no matter how serious the problem, the superintendent should seldom, if ever, leave the union with no acceptable way out. Individual(s) who are about to lose prestige with their peers become desperate and act in strange vindictive ways. It is never out of fashion to permit the union to save face.

Finally, the negotiation process deals with people more than situations. Thus, one must address people first. The people must be separated from the problem(s).

# CHAPTER 14

# The Superintendent as Communicator

Communication is involved in more than 90 percent of a superintendent's work time and is used while on the phone, at meetings and appointments, while writing letters and reports, etc. Using his appointment book as the source, one superintendent analyzed his work for each of five years and found that annually, he was involved in approximately 375 meetings and appointments. Communication was involved in all of these engagements. Thus, the superintendent as a communicator is a very important skill area.

As Kindred et al. (1984) note ". . . communication is a cooperative enterprise requiring the mutual interchange of ideas and information, and out of which understanding develops and action is taken" (p. 78). Thus, listening is also a part of communication.

In order to communicate effectively, a superintendent needs to know what, how, and with whom to communicate. This chapter is organized around these questions.

## WHAT DOES THE SUPERINTENDENT COMMUNICATE?

The subject of the communication is dependent upon the need and the group. Because many systems employ hundreds and sometimes thousands of individuals who work with hundreds or thousands of students who come from a community of hundreds or thousands, communication is the link that holds the system together and keeps it moving. Those involved in the school system, as well as those in the community, must be kept abreast of the system's operation including its plans, programs, personnel, etc. In addition, those within the system need to know about wages, benefits, and working conditions, and they also need to learn something about each other, especially if the system is large. Those in the community need to know about the goals, programs, services, and needs of the school system.

The linchpin of the communication function is the superintendent. Thus, it is the responsibility of the superintendent and staff to identify the communication needs of the various groups. This is done both by discussion and listening. After the needs are identified, the means to meet them and the persons to do so must be determined.

## HOW DOES THE SUPERINTENDENT COMMUNICATE?

### Verbal Communication

The superintendent communicates verbally in both oral and written form. Oral communication is done both formally and informally. Formally, the superintendent is often a presenter and at times, the featured speaker at meetings, conferences, banquets, graduations, etc., in addition to often being asked "to make a few remarks" at different occasions. Informally, business is transacted on the phone and through casual conversation.

On those occasions when the superintendent is asked in advance to make a presentation, time is needed for preparation. This preparation often means doing some reading of current literature and making notes. It also means organizing the presentation which involves developing an outline that presents the topic in a logical fashion. Writing, editing, and rewriting follow. It is helpful to have another individual, e.g., staff member, read and provide reaction to the concepts, presentation of the concepts, and format. The investment of time and energy in this effort says to the group to whom the presentation is delivered "this subject is important and you are important."

Even when the superintendent is asked "to make a few remarks," it is important to make notes so that what is said is coherent and has some meaning. Beware of off-the-cuff remarks. They often become a trap that ensnares the superintendent. Think before speaking.

The telephone is another important communication tool for the superintendent. The superintendent calls and is called by board members, staff, administrators, parents, business and community leaders, and many others. Much business is conducted via the telephone. Thus, one's choice of words and tone of voice as well as the content are critical for phone communication.

A suggestion regarding placing calls offered by a telephone company inservice person bears some consideration. It was suggested that one should place one's own calls rather than place calls through a secretary. In this context, if the superintendent does the calling, it says to the person receiving the call "you are important;" whereas, if the superintendent's secretary places the call and the superintendent gets on the line after the individual has been reached, that says to the person called "I am more important than you and my time is more valuable than yours." For the most part, people feel honored when receiving a call from the superintendent, especially when it's a direct call.

Another communication tool is the computer, particularly the personal computer equipped with a modem. This piece of hardware allows one to, via a telephone line, log onto a network and communicate throughout the network, between systems, across the state and nation and around the world. Software programs are available to assist the superintendent in word processing, graphics, accounting, etc. Computer literacy is an important communication skill for today's superintendent.

Written communication is also a significant part of a superintendent's work time. There are letters to be written to a myriad of people including administrators, teachers, parents, state agencies, community organizations, reports and proposals to the board, and newsletters to internal and external groups.

In order to meet the numerous written communication demands, a superintendent must have developed good writing skills. A poorly written communication, such as a letter, immediately creates an image of the superintendent as a less than professionally competent individual. Written communications must be thought out, organized, and clearly written. Sentences should be short and to the point and not compounded with several subordinate clauses. The vocabulary used should be understandable by the reader and should not include a lot of educational jargon. Finally, the communication should be neatly prepared. Computers and word processing software programs have made the preparation of written communication much easier.

## Nonverbal Communication

The superintendent communicates nonverbally through body language and appearance, the positions one takes sitting and standing can convey attentiveness, laziness, or lack of concern. For example, sitting slouched in a chair with one's feet extended and crossed can be read as "this is going too long. I'd better get comfortable." Facial expressions can be even more a display of one's attitude or feeling; a frown expresses displeasure, a smile acceptance. Eyes focused on the subject (person or action) indicate attentiveness, whereas eyes looking into the distance are often indicative of a lack of attention or concern or preoccupation with another topic.

Appearance is another form of communication. The superintendent should be dressed neatly and appropriately for the occasion. Neatness and appropriateness does not mean designer fashions. Grooming is equally important. Personal care conveys a message as well.

The superintendent's nonverbal communication, be it body language or appearance, should convey to those with whom contact is made that "this position is important and you are important." The superintendent, like it or not, is a model for others in the system.

## WITH WHOM DOES THE SUPERINTENDENT COMMUNICATE?

In order to answer this question, it is necessary to understand the term, *public*, because the superintendent serves many publics and must communicate with them. The concept of public comes from the area of marketing and is defined as "a distinct group of people and/or organizations that have an actual or a potential interest and/or impact on an organization" (Kotler, 1975, p. 17). For our purposes, publics are classified as internal and external. Internal publics are those individuals who work for the organization, and external publics are those individuals outside the organization who have an interest in or impact on the organization.

### Internal Publics

Internally, the superintendent communicates almost daily with the following groups:

1. *Board of education* that is the legally constituted policy-making body of the system
2. *Central office staff* which is or includes the system's top management team

3. *School administrators* who are the superintendent's links to and leaders of the system's schools
4. *Teachers* who are the front line staff in the teaching/learning process
5. *Support staff* who make the system function by their work as secretaries, custodians, janitors, food service personnel, classroom aides, etc.
6. *Students* who are the focus of the teaching/learning process

The superintendent communicates with these publics via many vehicles, such as newsletters, advisory committees, memoranda, and meetings and for many reasons, such as recognition of accomplishments, involvement in planning, improvement of working conditions, and orientation.

The formal communication with internal publics should be planned and such a plan should include the following:

1. The public to whom the communication is directed, e.g., administrators, teachers, students
2. The information to be communicated, e.g., curricular program change, staffing changes or assignments, new or pending legislation
3. The method of communication, e.g., newsletter, memo, letter, radio or television
4. The communicator, e.g., superintendent, board president, principal, community relations director
5. The timing of the communication, and if it is an ongoing communication such as a newsletter, the frequency

### External Publics

Among those groups with whom the superintendent communicates outside the school organization are the following:

1. *Parents* who share their children with schools and are the coeducators of their children. (The vehicle through which the superintendent often communicates is the Parent/Teacher or Home and School Association)
2. *Governmental bodies* such as the city or common council, the health department, fire and safety, public works, etc.

3. *Civic organizations* such as Rotary or Kiwanis who frequently have an interest in education and the community
4. *Religious organizations* that include churches, groups, clergy, etc.
5. *Special interest groups* who attempt to influence the school policy or organization
6. *Advisory committees* that are formed to address specific issues or concerns

The communication with external publics should also be planned, and the plan components are the same as those listed earlier for internal publics.

Finally, there is also another group which sometimes have been labeled *the crazies*. These are individuals who are the self-appointed superintendents and system critics and evaluators. They are often frequent letter writers or phone callers to the superintendent, the media, or anyone who will read or listen. Also, they are usually single issue people. Everything that happens has (or so they believe) some relevance to their issue. The superintendent must deal with these individuals. It's important to be courteous and helpful while at the same time being firm and conclusive.

## SUMMARY

The superintendent is a frequent, if not constant, communicator and must develop effective communication skills. S/he must know what is to be communicated, with whom to communicate, and how to communicate. The superintendent's image is often judged on the basis of the type and quality of her/his communication.

## REFERENCES

Kindred, L. W., D. Bagin and D. R. Gallagher (1984). *The School and Community Relations* (3rd edition). Englewood Cliffs, N.J.: Prentice-Hall.
Kotler, P. (1975). *Marketing for Nonprofit Organizations*. Englewood Cliffs, N.J.: Prentice-Hall.

# CHAPTER 15

# The Superintendent as Business Manager

The business management area is large and diverse. For example, Hill et al. (1982) list the following nineteen business management task areas that are applicable to any school system regardless of size or location:

1. Financial planning
2. Accounting
3. Debt service and capital fund management
4. Auditing
5. Purchasing and supply management
6. School plant planning and construction
7. Operation of plant
8. Maintenance of plant
9. Real estate management
10. Personnel management
11. Permanent property records and custody of legal papers
12. Transportation of pupils
13. Food service operations
14. Insurance
15. Cost analysis
16. Reporting
17. Collective bargaining

Dr. Thomas King provided helpful editing comments on this chapter. Dr. King is superintendent of the Ravenna City Schools in Ohio. He has a reputation as both an effective educational leader and an astute business manager.

18. Data processing
19. Board policies and administrative procedures as related to fiscal and noninstructional matters

Books have been written about each of these task areas. Thus, skill development in the business management area is beyond the scope of this chapter. Rather, this chapter discusses how a superintendent must relate to the business management area and identifies some business management knowledge that a superintendent must possess.

## A *MACRO* VIEW OF THE SUPERINTENDENT AS BUSINESS MANAGER

The business management area is probably the area in which most new superintendents feel the least competent. Perhaps it is no coincidence then that it is also the area that gets many superintendents into trouble.

Board members and citizens have a keen interest in the business management area, and there are several reasons for this interest. The first is historical in nature. Chapter 1 indicated that citizen involvement in education and in the superintendency itself has its roots in the business management area. Thus, there is a long-standing belief that business management should receive close oversight by the local citizenry. Second, business management task areas are tangible in nature. They represent things that can be counted, added, multiplied, bought, sold, etc. Third, money is a scarce educational resource. Many school systems receive a substantial portion of their financial support from local revenues. As a result, the citizens view the school board and superintendent as spending their money and consequently display concern that it be spent frugally and appropriately. Fourth, everyone has business management experience of some kind. There are personal budgets to be managed and purchases to be made. There are local businesses to be run. Is it little wonder then that business management concerns tend to occupy the major portion of many board meetings and receive extensive media attention.

In a small school system, the superintendent will be required to personally perform much of the business management detail work, with some help from principals and secretaries. In larger systems, professional help in the form of an assistant superintendent for business affairs, a business manager and/or a treasurer will be available to perform the detail work. However, by whatever means the work is performed, the superintendent must understand the various components well enough to use them appropriately in decision making; make explanations to the board, media, and citizens; and procure appropriate information for planning and reporting purposes. *Foulups* in the business management area will not be tolerated by the public. It is usually the superintendent's head that rolls in such instances.

The superintendent is the planning leader for the school system. At some point, all planning gets reduced to dollars and cents. Thus, if a superintendent does not understand the nuances of fiscal management and budgetary development, s/he, in essence, has delegated the planning function to those who do understand them.

The same can be said of decision making. If the superintendent has to ask someone if funds are, or can be made, available to hire additional teacher aides, repave the parking lot at the high school, or send some teachers and a principal to an educational conference, s/he has said to this *someone*, "Please make this decision for me." In the final analysis, the individual who makes the fiscal decisions also makes the educational decisions.

The trend toward empowering others to make significant educational decisions also means empowering them to make budgetary and expenditure decisions and causes interesting dilemmas as to how a superintendent empowers and still maintains appropriate systemwide fiscal accountability. The development of some innovative fiscal practices will be called for, and it is difficult to be fiscally innovative if one does not understand basic budgetary and accounting concepts.

The business management area poses a paradox for the superintendent. Seldom are superintendents hired primarily for their business management expertise, and seldom are they expected to spend a significant portion of their time on business management tasks. They are employed to be educational leaders, to raise student achievement scores, to improve school/community relations, etc. Business management tasks are but means to these ends, and as such, do not merit a lion's share of the superintendent's time. However, business management concerns tend to have an urgency about them and consequently, often do occupy much of a superintendent's time. Thus, it becomes imperative that a superintendent develop personal knowledge and skills in the business management task areas so that s/he can use them as they should be used, e.g., as support areas to the planning and educating functions. S/he must not become personally immersed in them to the extent that they become ends in and of themselves.

## A *MICRO* DISCUSSION OF THE SUPERINTENDENT AS BUSINESS MANAGER

In this section, eleven selected business management task areas are discussed as they relate to the superintendency.

### Financial Planning

The budget of a school system should reflect the educational goals of the district. This responsibility rests with the superintendent. S/he must be sure that the allocations to the various budget categories and line items do in fact reflect a proposed financial plan that supports and promotes the goals of the school system. This type of financial planning should take place on a strategic long-range basis as well as on an annual basis.

The superintendent is responsible for budget control. This means not just being sure that the system is living within its budget, but also that expenditures are being made that reflect the system's goals. For instance, if a new math curriculum is being implemented, then a series of expenditures by a principal in the English area should at least be questioned.

### Accounting

It is imperative that a superintendent know specifically what funds are included in each budget category and how these funds may be spent. It is also important to know how funds may be legally shifted between and among accounts. As emergencies and unforeseen needs appear throughout the year, the superintendent must be in a position to determine which needs take priority and to make decisions as to how these priority needs will be covered within the budget.

The superintendent must know the capabilities of the accounting system used in his/her system and devise ways to get maximum utilization from it. How can monthly revenues, expenditures, and encumbrances best be displayed for comparative and planning purposes? When does the system receive payments from the state foundation program and when does it receive its local property tax, sales tax, or income tax payments? How sophisticated is the accounting system with respect to the capability to calculate per instructional unit costs? If the superintendent knows the answers to these questions, s/he will have enhanced her/his decision-making capabilities.

A knowledge of how revenue flow correlates with expenditures will enable the superintendent to invest idle funds. Sometimes the investment of these funds for just a weekend can be worthwhile. The prudent short-term investment of funds is impressive to the board and community in addition to generating much needed revenue for the district.

Is the district taking advantage of discounts available for early payment of invoices? Having to pay an extra 5 percent because a payment is made two days late is an expenditure of funds that cannot be justified.

## Purchasing and Supply Management

A district can save a great deal of money with good purchasing and supply management procedures. Are complete specifications being developed prior to bidding? Are products tested prior to purchasing to make sure that they conform to specifications? Is bulk purchasing being optimally used? Could additional savings be rendered by joining with other systems in cooperative purchasing efforts? Are inventory procedures in place to ensure that supplies are being appropriately allocated and used? It is the superintendent's responsibility to see that someone is monitoring and trying to improve the purchasing and supply management process.

## School Plant Planning

Determining facility needs is extremely important. This entails performing demographic and student enrollment studies, and then applying the results of these studies to determine the best utilization of existing facilities. It is disastrous to close and sell a school facility and then have to go to the community five years later and ask for money to build a new one because enrollments have increased. On the other hand, it is difficult to justify keeping facilities open that are only partially filled because the per student cost of operating such facilities becomes inordinately high.

In situations calling for either facility renovation or new construction, it is important that educational specifications be developed prior to employing an architect. It is also important that the educational specifications be adequately communicated to the architect. The superintendent should insist on several schematics from the architect. Revising plans that the architect has used on another project seldom result in substantial financial savings to the district and often result in a design that does not adequately address the educational specifications.

The architect is the key to successful construction or renovation. Thoroughly check an architect's background. What other educational facilities has s/he done? What other projects does s/he currently have underway? Who will actually be doing the work on your project? Does the architect have a history of change orders? Does s/he adequately monitor the construction process? Too often, an architect is employed without a thorough background check.

## Plant Operation and Maintenance

The appearance of the school facilities and grounds is very influential in how the community views the schools. Windows broken and unpainted, bushes untrimmed, and litter around the grounds show a lack of pride. In addition to the enhancement of school community relations through good operation and maintenance practices, some effective schools research has indicated that these practices also are correlated with higher student achievement levels.

The operation and maintenance personnel need to be inserviced so that they complement the educational program. Their schedules should be adjusted to the program and not vice versa. They should be treated as important people within the school organization.

When funds are tight, it often is maintenance that gets postponed. Roof and parking lot repairs, painting, and preventive maintenance activities can be postponed for one more year. Sometimes it is necessary to do these things; however, this is often penny-wise and pound-foolish. For instance, roof and window replacements that resulted from deferred maintenance are much more costly than the preventive maintenance would have been. Sometimes decisions not to postpone maintenance are very difficult ones, particularly when the teachers are pushing for raises and funds are not available.

## Personnel Management

Records are extremely important in this area. Accuracy and currency are a necessity. This is an area on which the superintendent probably will spend little personal time, but one in which s/he will pay a big price if there is a mistake.

The appropriate selection, training, and supervision of noninstructional staff is often not given the attention it deserves. In addition to providing important services, these individuals can be very effective goodwill ambassadors for the schools.

## Pupil Transportation

Policies, rules, regulations, and procedures are very important in pupil transportation. Parents get very concerned over such seemingly minor things as changing the pickup or drop-off location for their child by a block or several hundred yards.

A superintendent of a small district can find himself/herself devoting much of his/her personal time to transportation. Problems in this area can have significant negative public relations consequences and thus cannot be ignored or delegated carelessly.

One may be called upon to make recommendations on contract versus district-owned equipment. There are pros and cons to both sides. A very thorough investigation should be performed before any recommendations are made.

## Food Service Operation

In many school systems, the number of school lunches served on any given day surpasses the total number of meals served in all the restaurants in town. An operation of this magnitude obviously must be well-managed fiscally. In addition, lunchroom workers who are rude to students, a shortage of food, inappropriately prepared food, etc. can cause public relation problems.

Most systems have a goal of making the cafeterias self-supporting. Sometimes the cafeteria managers take pride not in just breaking even financially but in making money. The superintendent must make sure the food service operation is fiscally sound, provides nutritious and tasty meals, promotes a good image of the school, and also is looked upon by the food service personnel in a proper perspective. In other words, the food service operation is for the benefit of the students and the educational program and does not have entrepreneurship as a primary objective.

## Insurance

It is necessary for school systems to purchase a number of insurance policies. This is a complex and costly endeavor. There must be constant monitoring to assure that the coverages are appropriate and that they are being purchased for the best possible price.

As mentioned, insurance has become very complex. It is necessary to get the advice of specialists both in determining insurance needs and in analyzing policies. Chapter 17 addresses the important, but difficult, task of working with specialists.

## Collective Negotiations

Directly negotiating with noncertified personnel has become as big an issue in many systems as negotiating with certificated personnel. One must be careful to maintain educational flexibility in negotiating a contract with noncertified personnel. The educational program should not be curtailed because of contract limitations in such areas as working hours, job responsibilities, supervisory authority, etc.

In all negotiations, it is important to have accurate and timely information. It is important that the cost of any proposal put on the table be accurately projected. Any hidden costs should be identified. Again, the superintendent may not have the direct responsibility for doing the projecting, but s/he will be the one who will bear the brunt of any miscalculations.

## Data Processing

This is the last selected task area to be discussed, but perhaps it is the one that presents the greatest decision-making difficulty for the superintendent. With computer hardware available that can store vast amounts of data and perform an almost unlimited number of calculations in an unbelievably short time, the superintendent is faced with a number of crucial decisions. One of the most difficult is to determine the district needs. Due to advancements in both hardware and software, a vast array of data analyzing alternatives are available that heretofore were nonexistent. Even with the help of specialists, it is difficult to get a handle on all of the possibilities.

When system needs have been determined, hardware decisions have to be made. Should some activities, such as payroll, be contracted out? Should hardware be purchased or leased? How actively should the system get into developing its own software? Decisions on these matters are not cast in granite. However, due to substantial capital outlays and extensive personnel training necessitated by decisions in this area, a school system is bound by its decisions for a period of years.

## CONCLUDING COMMENTS

To be an effective educational leader, a superintendent must also be an effective business manager. It is through the business management task areas that the school organization is made to function efficiently and funds are appropriated and expended in such a way that the achievement of the system's goals is optimized.

The business management area can be a source of frustration for a superintendent. It is a diverse and complex area that must be handled accurately and astutely and, consequently, can become very demanding on a superintendent's time. However, it is a support area to the educational leadership function and must be treated accordingly. It is essential that a superintendent constantly monitor the allocation of his/her time between business management activities and other vital educational leadership-related demands.

The size of the school system generally determines how much business management detail work the superintendent personally must perform. However, in any system, the superintendent must be familiar with the many and sundry aspects of business management and use them innovatively and advantageously in the educational leadership process.

In preparing for a superintendency, one should seek opportunities for exposure to the business management side of school operations. No internship in the superintendency should be devoid of such exposure.

In conclusion, a superintendent must not be overwhelmed by the business management aspects of operating a school system. Providing leadership for educational planning and effective instruction should always be the top priorities.

## REFERENCE

Hill, F. W. et al. (1982). *A special committee report sponsored by the ASBO board of directors on the qualifications and responsibilities of the school business administrator*; (Bulletin No. 21, Third Edition). Park Ridge, Ill.: The Research Corporation of the Association of School Business Officials.

# CHAPTER 16

# The Superintendent as Lobbyist

One can no longer be an effective superintendent by just minding the store at the local level. One must work to become influential in educational matters at the state level, and on occasion, at the national level. With many public school districts receiving over 50 percent of their funds from the state and with all districts being directly subjected to state control via state level legislation and administrative mandates, it is extremely important that a superintendent work to exert influence at the state-level in a way that will benefit education in general and one's own district in specific.

Often, superintendents who do make an effort to be influential at the state level confine their efforts to executive branch bureaucracts because these individuals develop the guidelines for implementing newly enacted legislation. However, to focus one's efforts in this manner ignores a coequal branch of government, the legislature. It is in the legislature that basic policy affecting education is forged. It is in the legislative arena that superintendents are finding it increasingly necessary to be active. In other words, superintendents must now be competent lobbyists on behalf of education and their school systems. Quite simply, lobbying has become one of the most effective ways of fulfilling one's system's needs.

The lobbying effort is performed as an individual on behalf of one's local system and at times as part of an educational coalition with mutual interests. The larger the represented group, the greater the power base.

Mr. Warren Russell provided the basic material for this chapter. Mr. Russell has served for eleven years as a full-time lobbyist; seven years for the Buckeye Association of School Administrators, which is the state association for superintendents; and four years at the Ohio Department of Education. He is viewed by legislators as a very reliable lobbyist and an extremely influential advocate for education.

Being an effective lobbyist presents another dimension to the super-intendency. Lobbying means interacting with noneducators who often will have divergent ideas about what is good for education. Partisan politics and competition with competing interest groups become a reality. The legislative process itself is complex and difficult to comprehend. Foes one day will be allies the next. Legislators will shift their stances on issues overnight. One could go on with the interesting, and at times frustrating, vagaries in the life of a lobbyist. It is a process with which most superintendents have had limited experience. Thus, the object of this chapter is to identify some basic guidelines to start one on the route to becoming an influential lobbyist. It should be noted that these guidelines are just the beginning, for becoming an effective lobbyist is a time-consuming and ongoing task.

In the interests of brevity, much of the information that follows is presented in list form.

## CONTACTING LEGISLATORS

### General Guidelines

When communicating with your legislator, the following general guidelines will be helpful:

1. Provide factual information on the subject that supports your position. Do not do such things as demand support, make threats, present unfounded allegations, become emotional, or express indignation. Emotional responses are usually not heard.

2. In explaining the problem or issue remember that the legislator is probably not an educator; thus, avoid the use of educational jargon. Such language will confuse — not impress — your legislator.

3. Honor any reasonable request made by your legislator for information that s/he may need on educational issues. Respond in a timely and concise fashion.

4. Express your views promptly on any pending legislation so that your position will be considered along with the other opinions that your legislator will receive.

5. Do not concern yourself with the legislator's party affiliation.

Most legislation that directly affects the public schools will be decided on its merits as opposed to party line philosophies.

6. Know your legislator. What are your legislator's outlooks, aspirations, and problems? Formulate your arguments, and arrange and present your facts accordingly. Often a cost/benefit ratio is an approach worth considering.

7. Remember that legislators try to represent all their constituents. Recognize the fact that there are legitimate differences of opinion that will necessitate the legislator to compromise or contradict your position on occasion. Therefore, when formulating your reaction to a situation, try to understand the motivations and thinking of others who do not agree with your position.

8. Be sure to thank and commend your legislator for the helpful things s/he does. Let your legislator know that you are aware of and appreciate the work and support s/he has put forth on behalf of your position.

9. Maintain contact with your legislators throughout the year. Do not contact them only when you need their help. Keep them informed. Invite them to tour your schools.

10. If a certain legislator has been particularly helpful, give him/her your support in his/her effort to gain reelection. This help can be either monetary or a volunteering of your time. Superintendents typically remain aloof in reelection campaigns. Of course, there are legitimate arguments for not becoming involved in some partisan campaigns. However, do not remain noncommittal on the sidelines while a particularly effective legislator for education gets defeated.

11. Usually it is best not to ask legislators to introduce legislation. Coalitions and professional associations are usually more effective at this. There may be an occasion when your association asks for your assistance with your legislator regarding the introduction of legislation.

## Personal Contacts

A well-planned personal conversation with a legislator is almost always the preferred course of action. During the legislative session, legislators are extremely busy, so make the most of the opportunity to meet with your legislator however brief it may be.

1. The first step is to get an appointment. You can try for a personal appointment; however, you will probably have to go through an appointment secretary. Appointment secretaries have a tremendous amount of influence over who gets to see the legislator. Getting to know the appointment secretary is usually time well spent.

2. When attempting to get an appointment, give your name, indicate if you are a constituent, indicate your primary interest in meeting with the legislator, and offer two or three alternative times you are available for a meeting.

3. Unless you are a personal friend of the legislator, address a representative as *Mr./Ms.* and a senator as *Senator*.

4. It is often advisable to take a colleague along to the meeting.

5. Be prepared when you arrive. Know the bill you want to discuss and what you want to say about it. Have accurate facts to support your position. Offer a solution to the problem that is win-win for both you and the legislator.

6. After the meeting, send a thank-you letter. If you promised to furnish the legislator with some written information, now is the time to do it.

## Written Correspondence

If you are not able to contact your legislator personally, letter writing is the next best approach. By following a few simple guidelines, it can be an effective approach.

1. Always correspond with your legislator and the appropriate committee chairperson. As a matter of courtesy, your legislator should be copied on all correspondence to other members of the legislature. On federal matters, limit your letters to members of your state delegation in the U.S. Congress and Senate and write your representative and senators first. As a matter of congressional courtesy, all letters written by non-constituents are referred to the proper congressman for a reply. It usually is advisable to copy your professional association on any correspondence with legislators at either the state or federal level.

Address correspondence to any legislator at either the state or federal level to *The Honorable John/Jane Doe.*

Correspondence with legislators should be sent to the following addresses:

*U.S. Senator*
United States Senate
New Senate Office Bldg.
Washington, D.C. 20515

*U.S. Congressman*
House of Representatives
House Office Bldg.
Washington, D.C. 20515

*State Senator*
(Name of State) Senate
(State Capitol), (State)
  (Zip Code)

*State Representative*
(Name of State) House of
  Representatives
(State Capitol), (State)
  (Zip Code)

2. Be sure your letter is timely. Preferably, write just prior to committee hearings that will address your area of concern, and again, just prior to a vote on the issue.
3. Avoid form letters. They are easily recognized by legislators and have little impact. Letters expressing your own thoughts in your own words are what legislators want to read.
4. Some specifics of letter writing are as follows:
   • Clarity and conciseness are essential.
   • Type the letter and use your own or your district's stationery.
   • Identify yourself and briefly state your purpose for writing.
   • Limit your letter to one specific subject, indicate what the issue is, and identify the bill by author, number, and subject.
   • Make your point in the first paragraph. Use the remainder of the letter to explain and support your view.
   • Personalize your argument. Give examples to illustrate your point and how the legislation would affect your school district.
   • Always provide accurate information.
   • Indicate that your system serves *x* number of the legislator's constituents.
   • Be polite. Reason works better than coercion. Don't demand his/her vote. Ask for it.
5. Say "Thank you" when it is deserved.

## TESTIFYING AT LEGISLATIVE HEARINGS

Testifying before a legislative committee can be a very rewarding experience. However, if you are unfamiliar with the hearing process, the following suggestions will be helpful:

1. The first requirement is that you be completely familiar with the bill currently being discussed. Know what the opponents as well as the proponents of the bill are saying.

2. Learn something of the district represented by each committee member. This will assist in anticipating questions and in understanding each member's frame of reference when asking questions.

3. It is necessary to register with the committee before you testify. The committee chair will have witness slips available for completion.

4. When beginning your testimony, acknowledge the chair and committee members as follows: "Chair (name) and members of the (name of committee) committee."

5. Identify yourself and your mission in the following manner: "My name is (name) and I am testifying in support (or opposition) to House Bill (or Senate Bill) (bill number). I am the superintendent of the (name of school district)."

6. If at all possible, do not read from a written statement—summarize and paraphrase. Take no more than seven to ten minutes to present your testimony. Highlight the key issues in your testimony. Describe your positions, issues, and concerns clearly and succinctly. Don't duck the issues. Make a concise statement describing central problems and your expert proposal for resolving them.

7. Use accurate data and examples to illustrate your points where appropriate. If you have charts, graphs, or other complex data to present, pass out copies before you testify.

8. If you wish to refer to particular parts of the bill, do so by line number(s).

9. If you wish to distribute written copies of your testimony, it is usually best to do so after you have testified.

10. Following your testimony, the committee members may question you. Respond only to those questions for which you have

answers, experience, knowledge, or considered opinions. Do not be reluctant to say, "I don't know." Don't try to fake it.

11. Don't interrupt a committee member when s/he is asking a question or making a statement.

12. Don't argue with a committee member. If you disagree, courteously indicate such, state your case, and say no more.

13. Speak slowly, distinctly, and loud enough to be heard by all committee members.

14. Don't be alarmed if legislators leave the room during your testimony. Often many committees meet at the same time, and legislators frequently have to move from one committee to another.

15. At the close of the your testimony, thank the chair and the committee members for the opportunity to testify.

16. Immediately followup with any additional information that you may have agreed to furnish the committee.

## POTPOURRI OF LOBBYING TIPS

Some specific pointers have been put forth in the preceding sections relative to contacting legislators and testifying at legislative hearings. This section includes a score of general suggestions for improving your lobbying effectiveness. Some of the suggestions will be more apropos for you than others. Use those that can benefit you.

1. Know how a bill becomes law. You must know the process before you can effectively use it to your advantage.

2. Be current on issues that interest you. When the legislature is in session, professional associations usually publish a weekly status update of pending legislation that could potentially affect education. Loiter around the legislative halls and listen more than you talk. Legislators like to talk; take advantage of this trait. You need all the information you can obtain.

3. Usually the best thing you have to offer a legislator is information; thus, be prepared. Do your homework.

4. Always be objective and tell the truth—all of it. Learn to say, "I don't know, but I'll find out." Once personal credibility is lost, the return road is a long one. In the final analysis, the essence of lobbying is credibility. Don't lose it!

5. Don't mix facts and personal bias without explaining which is which. Along this same line, don't operate on assumptions and don't get caught up in too much speculation.

6. Always be on time with material. Provide sufficient background information. Legislator knowledge of important background information cannot be assumed.

7. Identify your priorities. Identify one or two major issues and pursue them diligently. Don't confuse minor issues with major ones.

8. With any issue, know what you are willing to settle for. Understand the art of compromise, trade-offs, and coalitions.

9. Deal with issues not personalities. Personalizing is dangerous. Your adversary today very likely may be your ally tomorrow.

10. Some people in the legislative process at any given time will be more important to you than others; however, don't burn any bridges. In this day and age, legislators and aides tend to be around government in various capacities for a long time.

11. Relate to legislators from both political parties.

12. Whenever possible, form coalitions. The larger the constituent base you are representing, the greater your power.

13. Recognize the politics of issues. Remember that legislators have a number of different constituencies.

14. Know as much about key legislators as you can. Study their voting records. What are their basic philosophic beliefs? Who are the prominent constituent groups in their districts? Who contributed money and time to election and reelection efforts? What kinds of advice are the legislators receiving from their aides?

15. Maintain consistent contact with your legislators and other key legislators. Provide assistance whenever possible.

16. Always follow through on a promise.

17. Don't leave a legislator hanging by switching positions on an issue.

18. Always try to share the glory with a legislator. Never embarrass one or make a member of his/her staff look bad.

19. Never bad-mouth another legislator.

20. Always remember to say "Thank you." Put it in writing.

## CONCLUDING COMMENTS

Develop your own unique lobbying style by integrating the suggestions in this chapter with your personal strengths and experiences. Being an effective lobbyist is no longer an occasional concern for a superintendent. It has become an integral part of the superintendency. Learn how to lobby well and also have fun while doing it. No matter what happens in one legislative session, another one will follow.

# CHAPTER 17

# The Superintendent as Consulter of Specialists

Beginning with the passage of the Occupational Safety and Health Act of 1970 and the National Environmental Policy Act of 1970, state and federal regulation of safety, health, and environmental practices has proliferated to the point that virtually every aspect of a private employer's safety, health, and environmental practices is controlled. In recent years, a very clear trend of increasing governmental regulation of the public employer has developed. As a result, public employers are also now subject to a number of federal environmental regulations, such as Title III of the Superfund Amendments and Reauthorization Act (SARA–Title III), the Underground Storage Tank (UST) Regulations, and the Asbestos Hazard Emergency Response Act (AHERA).

To date, there has been little regulation of the public sector in the safety and health areas. However, major public sector unions currently are giving high priority to the passage of public sector safety and health legislation. They are also pushing to have safety and health provisions included in collective bargaining agreements. These areas require specialists.

Additional examples of the impact of specialists on the school system are numerous. For instance, the various types of insurance coverage schools must purchase have become complicated enough to require the advice of specialists. If one is renovating or constructing new facilities, one must rely on the recommendations of engineering firms and architects. It is a rare school system that does not have a lawyer on retainer. The recommendations of school psychologists have become very influential in the special education arena.

The list of specialists with whom the superintendent must interact on a daily basis is lengthy. Unless handled properly, these specialists will in fact become the decision makers for the school system. Their recommendations will supplant the decision making of the superintendent and his/her staff. Then, the specialists become substitutes for superintendent leadership. However, it is possible to interact with these specialists, assimilate and use their information, and still retain the leadership and decision-making reins of the school system. The purpose of this chapter is to offer suggestions as to how this can be done.

The next section addresses positive ways to interact with specialists. This is followed by a section on the appropriate use of consultants. The superintendent has complete control over who s/he employs as a consultant, which is not the case with other specialists with whom the superintendent must interact. Thus, selection of the most appropriate consultants and the conditions of their employment are factors that can and should be controlled by the superintendent.

## INTERACTING WITH SPECIALISTS

The objective of using specialists is to get them to serve the school system but not to control it. The first rule of thumb is to confine the specialists to their areas of expertise. There is a tendency for specialists to go beyond their areas of expertise and offer personal opinions under the guise of professional advise. For instance, a lawyer, instead of informing you as to what the law specifically allows or does not allow, will offer an opinion as to what s/he believes your decision should be. The lawyer may indicate that a student should be given another chance, not because the law indicates that the student is entitled to another chance, but because s/he personally believes it would be a desirable thing to do. In other words, instead of providing you with a set of viable options, s/he has attempted to make a decision for you.

To avoid having specialists substitute their judgment for that of the superintendent, one should decide a desirable course of action, and then, using the example of the attorney, say to him/her "This is what I want to do; how can I do it?" instead of asking him/her "Can I do this?" There are always reasons why something cannot be done. Teach the school staff to interact with specialists in a similar manner. Otherwise, the staff members will allow the specialists to make decisions for them, and in the process, for the superintendent and the school system.

If a law or policy is being put forth as the basis for a specialist's recommendation, ask for a copy of the law or policy in question. Study it. What does it really say? Assign staff members the responsibility for becoming knowledgeable in specific specialty areas. Ask questions, ask questions, and then ask some more questions. What if we do this? Why do things have to be done this way? What would prohibit us from taking another course of action?

Some government bureaucrats who are imposed on the schools will probably resist this probing at first through verbal intimidation tactics, but a calm unemotional pursuit of the issue will bring results. However, it must be added, this can be a delicate situation, particularly with local officials with whom you must interact on a continuing basis or who might be politically influential. These situations call for exceptionally good interpersonal relations skills as well as persistency.

Check with other superintendents about advice they have received and how they have dealt with similar situations. The superintendent should not feel that s/he has to rely solely on a specialist's advice.

In summary, if specialists know that the superintendent is going to be inquisitive and do homework on his/her own, one generally will receive more thoughtful and reliable advice from them. No professional likes to appear unprepared in his/her area of expertise.

## THE APPROPRIATE USE OF CONSULTANTS

The term *consultants* refers to individuals that a superintendent employs to perform a specific task(s) because s/he has a special need for their expertise. A plan outlining the appropriate use of consultants can be very helpful to a superintendent. When a superintendent has a problem with a consultant, it is usually because enough thought and effort did not go into defining the need for the consultant, the selection of the consultant, and/or the conditions of employment. Thus, each of these important aspects will be addressed individually in the sections that follow. The superintendent has complete control over who is employed as a consultant and the conditions of employment and should take full advantage of these options.

### Need for a Consultant

A superintendent should first determine with the staff and the board the specific problem(s) that needs to be addressed. For instance, if facility utilization appears to be a problem, information on student and community demographics, enrollment projections, and facility analyses must be obtained. Decisions must them be made on which of these things can be done in-house and which, if any, call for the services of a consultant.

Once a problem has been identified, the decision regarding the hiring of a consultant usually depends upon the expertise available on staff, the time available for staff members to devote to the problem(s), and/or the credibility that might be gained by receiving a report from an unbiased outside source.

If expertise is not available on staff, then obviously some form of outside help is needed. However, often expertise is available on staff, but time to devote to the problem is not. For instance, a good demographic study requires a considerable amount of time and effort. If all of the central office administrators are overcommitted already, to ask one of them to take on the task would mean that their other important leadership responsibilities would be put on hold. Often, it is not in the best interests of the school system to reallocate their time to address the problem. Lastly, changes in facility utilization policies usually mean some students will be transferred to other schools. This, in turn, means that a number of parents are going to be upset, and that the motives and wisdom of the superintendent and board will come into question. An outside consultant can add credibility to data that are generated and can help *take some of the heat* as well.

### Consultant Selection

As with the employment of any personnel, there is no substitute for time spent performing a thorough background check. Competent individuals that one wants to hire as consultants have an established reputation. Check their record. Do their projects come in on time? Are their reports meticulously done, and do they provide supporting data to back up conclusions, recommendations, and alternatives? Do they display good interpersonal relations skills when working with the staff and community? And, most importantly, do their projections and conclusions withstand the test of time? In other words, do they have a history of success?

Do not be bashful to ask consultants to submit copies of reports generated for other jobs. Check with other systems who have employed them for work similar to what you want them to do.

Be sure that it is known who will actually be doing the work. Will assistants, or in the case of university personnel, graduate assistants, be one the ones actually collecting the data? How many other projects will the consultants have in progress at the time your job is being done? Will they have an ample amount of time to devote to your project?

After all the background and reference checks have turned out positive, there still is an element of art in the final selection. The superintendent should feel comfortable with the consultant. A certain positive chemistry should exist, but if it doesn't, be wary about employing the individual(s).

There are two situations that should raise a red flag. First, beware of the *indispensable* consultant. A good consultant should phase out of a project. Second, do not allow a situation to develop where a consultant may realize a personal monetary gain as a result of a particular recommendation. For example, a case can be made that the attorney who recommends that a school system pursue a resolution to a problem through the courts should not be the attorney who will represent the system in court. The recommendation to go to court may be a solid one and made in good faith, but a doubt still lingers if the recommending attorney stands to receive a healthy fee for representing the school system in the court proceedings.

### Contracting with a Consultant

It is essential to communicate to the consultant the type of report desired and the things that should be included in the report. For instance, facts should be clearly differentiated from opinions and projections. Background information and assumptions upon which projections and recommendations are based should be included in the report. It also is important, when feasible, to ask the consultant to present a list of alternatives with the pros and cons of each alternative listed. This approach leaves the superintendent and board with the final responsibility for selecting a course of action, which is as it should be.

After the details have been agreed upon with the consultant, a written contract should be developed. The contract should be detailed and specific, in writing, and approved by the board. Memories are short on the specifics of employment. As time elapses, disagreement can arise over the specifics of the services to be rendered. A detailed written contract greatly decreases the probability of such a misunderstanding. A clear contract is helpful to both parties.

A contract can be very legalistic in nature, but it does not have to be. More importantly, it should include the specific objectives of the consulting project, the responsibilities of the employing school system, the responsibilities of the consultant, a timetable for completion of the project, the project cost, and method of payment. A sample contract of this nature follows.

---

### A PROPOSAL TO PROJECT STUDENT ENROLLMENTS AND PROVIDE FACILITY UTILIZATION ALTERNATIVES FOR THE A-ONE SCHOOLS

#### I. GENERAL COMMENTS AND ORGANIZATION OF PROPOSAL

This proposal is submitted at the request of the Board of Education and Superintendent of the A-One Schools. Its general purposes are to collect and analyze data, and subsequently, to formulate enrollment projections, determine facility capacities, and provide facility utilization alternatives. The proposal is organized as follows:

A. Objectives of the study
B. Responsibilities of the A-One Schools
C. Responsibilities of the project director
D. Timetable for completion of the project
E. Project cost

#### II. OBJECTIVES OF THE STUDY

The proposal is designed to address the following objectives:

A. Determine the educational design capacity and general condition of each facility
B. Project student enrollments through 1997
C. Provide alternatives for housing the anticipated student enrollments

In order to fulfill the objectives put forth above, the project director will use on-site visitations; interviews with appropriate educational, community, and business leaders; as well as data provided by school personnel, city officials, and other agencies in the city. The assumptions and methods of data analysis used in formulating each projection or alternative will be presented.

#### III. RESPONSIBILITIES OF THE A-ONE SCHOOLS

The A-One Schools will provide the following data to the project director:

A. Schematic drawings of each facility and addition

B. Construction dates for each facility and addition

C. Interior space usage information for each facility, i.e., number of classrooms and offices, average square footage per classroom, etc. (Forms will be furnished by the project director.)

D. Site data, i.e., acreage, restrictions, drainage problems, etc.

E. Map(s) showing the current school attendance boundaries

F. Data on any special instructional programs currently housed in any of the facilities, i.e., nature of the programs and number enrolled

G. Enrollments by grade level by school for the past nine years. Any changes in attendance areas during this period of time should be identified. (Forms will be furnished by the project director.)

H. Number of tuition students by grade level in each facility for the current year

I. Data on students attending private or parochial schools, i.e., number, grade level, and attendance areas in which residing

J. Data on students attending school(s) in another district

K. Current board policy for the assignment of students to schools

L. Current board policy on class size

M. Itemized operating and maintenance costs for each facility for the last five years

N. Itemized listing of major capital expenditures for each facility for the last ten years by year and dollar amount

O. Copies of any studies performed relative to student demographic and/or enrollment trends or facility utilization

P. Copies of any documents containing data relative to city demographic trends

## IV. RESPONSIBILITIES OF THE PROJECT DIRECTOR

In order to accomplish the objectives of the proposal, the project director assumes the following responsibilities:

A. Gathering of all information relevant to the proposal except that outlined in the preceding section

B. Analysis of all information

C. Development of relevant projections and alternatives

D. Compilation of a written report

E. Providing the board and superintendent with fifteen copies of the written report

F. An oral presentation of the written report to the board and superintendent

G. Travel costs

H. Data analysis costs

I. Costs associated with producing the written report

J. Costs of additional professional help that the project director may deem necessary for the successful completion of
the project

## V. TIMETABLE FOR COMPLETION OF THE PROJECT

Upon adoption of this proposal by the board of education, the project
director will provide to the board and superintendent fifteen copies of the
written report in January of 19___ if the information in Section III is made
available by September 1, 19___. The oral presentation to the board and
superintendent will be made at this time or, at the discretion of the board, will
be made on a mutually agreeable later date.

## VI. PROJECT COST

The project will be undertaken as presented in this document for a total
cost to the A-One Board of Education of $X$ dollars ($ $X$). $Y$ dollars ($ $Y$) will be
due on November 1, 19___. The remaining $Z$ dollars ($ $Z$) will be due when
the fifteen copies of the written report are submitted to the Board and superintendent.

The above amounts are payable to the project director, Connie Consultant, at the following address:

> Connie Consultant
> Honorarium Ave.
> Demographic City, Any State 99999

> *Respectfully submitted,*

> Connie Consultant
> Project Director

# PART THREE

# Preparing for, Obtaining, and Departing "A Superintendency"

Aspiring to and learning about the superintendency are academic exercises unless one is knowledgeable about the processes of preparing for and obtaining one. This subdivision addresses these key processes.

After one has *superintended* for a number of years, a feeling of being *trapped* in the position sometimes sets in. Professionally viable alternatives to the superintendency do not seem to be available. Also, with the advent of earlier retirements, many individuals wish to remain professionally productive and active but are at a loss as to how to do so. This subdivision addresses this career change dilemma that superintendents are experiencing with greater frequency.

# CHAPTER 18

# Preparation for and Initiation into a Superintendency

An individual's preparation for and initiation into the super-intendency is both formal and informal and occurs both prior to and after assumption of the position. The formal and informal preparation and initiation processes are grounded in socialization theory. Thus, the chapter begins with a brief review of socialization literature in order to set the stage for the discussions on formal and informal preparation and initiation that follow.

## SOCIALIZATION THEORY

Socialization is the process by which a role aspirant learns the values, norms, requisite work skills and abilities, and required behavior for a specific role (Clausen, 1968). According to Baldwin (1969), the principal components of socialization theory are internalization, identity, significant others, role learning, and process. A brief discussion of each of these components follows.

With respect to the first component, it is important that one identifies and internalizes the values and norms that are shared by those in the group to which one aspires or has joined and which are expected for a particular role (Spencer and Inkeles, 1976). This belief does not mean that the individual has to blindly accept all standards and may never question them.

Second, during the socialization process one assumes an identity, in this case the role of superintendent. The aspirant begins to take on the values, norms, and behavior of a superintendent and develops an identity with it. Internalization and identification occur together.

The third integral component is what Mead (1934) calls the "significant other." Significant others are those persons "who have great influence because of their frequency of contact, their primacy, and their control over rewards and punishment" (Brim and Wheeler, 1966, p.8). The significant other may be a group as well as an individual and is sometimes referred to as the socializing agent. Mentors and sponsors are examples of significant others. It is the role, behavior, attitudes, and values of the significant others that are taken on by the one being socialized.

The fourth component is role learning. A role, according to Sarbin and Allen (1968), "is an organized set of behaviors that belongs to an identifiable position, and these behaviors are activated when the position is occupied" (pp. 545-546). Thus, to perform the superintendent's role satisfactorily, the aspirant must know what is expected and be willing to meet those expectations.

The superintendency role expectations are the specifications established for that position by the individual occupying it and by others who interact with it. Those expectations "define the limits or range of tolerated behavior" (Sarbin and Allen, 1968, p. 501) and comprise "the rights and privileges, the duties and obligations, of (that position) in relation to other positions" (p. 487) in the educational and community structure.

Another type of role learning is modeling. A role model is an individual whose "behaviors, personal styles, and specific attributes are emulated by others" (Shapiro et al., 1978, p. 52). According to Bandura (1977) "most behavior is learned observationally through modeling" (p. 22). In modeling, an individual observes behavior, mentally codes it, and later recalls it for performance use. An important plus of modeling is its multiplicative power because a single model can transmit behavior to several individuals.

Before leaving this discussion of role learning, it is important to note that cultural learning is also important. Culture applies to the organization or institution. "An organization . . . has a personality of sorts, often referred to as an organizational culture . . . (which) conveys important assumptions and norms governing membership, values, activities, and aims" (Louis, 1980, p. 232). The new superintendent, then, must learn who's who and what's what in the system and community in order to function effectively.

The fifth and final element of socialization concerns the process. The socialization process is continuous and interactional. It is a two-way process involving the *socializee* and the *socializer(s)*. An individual is not socialized for a role that is then performed unchangingly. There is interaction with others and that interaction contributes to the continued socialization.

The socialization process is divided into two principal types, primary and secondary, and these are further segmented into formal and informal. Primary socialization is that socialization an individual experiences in childhood and through which one becomes a member of society. Secondary socialization "is any subsequent process that inducts an already socialized individual into new sectors of the objective world of his/her society" (Berger and Luckman, 1967, p. 130).

Distinguishing factors between formal and informal socialization are the role of the learner and the material to be learned. Greenfield (1985) notes that "in formal socialization . . . both the role of the learner and the material to be learned are specified . . . (whereas in) informal neither . . . are specified in an explicit, formal sense" (p. 100). Formal socialization processes are found in seminaries, military training, medical schools, and graduate schools. Informal socialization includes that which Wolcott (1973) calls "conventional wisdom," i.e., the verbal and informal transmission of an oral literature accumulated through years of experience and passed on to succeeding generations primarily by the peer group.

Socialization also occurs in two stages, before and after assuming the role. That which takes place before role assumption is labeled anticipatory, and the learning that occurs after role assumption is called encounter.

## FORMAL PREPARATION AND INITIATION

Formally, a person aspiring to the superintendency is expected to secure state certification for the position. While the specific requirements differ from state to state, there are three general requirements: (1) satisfactory completion of specified graduate coursework and/or degrees (usually a minimum of a master's degree is required), (2) satisfactory completion of one or more internships, and (3) evidence of satisfactory performance in another administrative position within a school system. Upon satisfactory completion of the above requirements, the state department of education issues the applicant a provisional certificate for a specified number of years. Usually graduate coursework and/or other professional development activities are required for renewal of the certificate.

In graduate school programs and courses, aspiring superintendents are exposed to the relevant knowledge, skills, and thought processes, as well as to the expected norms and behavior that are associated with the superintendency. They also begin to develop an image or understanding of the role and its demands.

One or more internships are required for certification. Today, most states have increased the intensity and/or duration of the internship during which the intern is expected to devote at least a semester, and often a year, working under the supervision of a practicing superintendent and university professor. Here, one assists in many of the superintendent's tasks and is gradually given responsibility for some of them. In this way, the person begins to make the transition from theory to practice and *gets a feel for the position*.

Following employment, a new superintendent is engaged in a second and somewhat less formal socialization process that consists of an orientation program introducing the individual to the system. The content of the program usually includes an introduction to or review of the system's philosophy, objectives, mission statement, and organization. There is also an introduction to the central office staff, building-level administrators, faculty, support staff, and key community leaders.

## INFORMAL PREPARATION AND INITIATION

As noted in the theory section, there is an informal socialization process, the passing on of *conventional wisdom* and role modeling. This informal process may be even more influential than the formal process discussed in the preceding section. It is a process that does not stop with the acquisition of a superintendency. In fact, many of the informal socialization processes continue uninterrupted as one makes the step from an aspiring to a practicing superintendent. As such, the informal socialization of aspiring and practicing superintendents will be treated together.

Practicing superintendents and professors with superintendency experience share their experiences with aspirants and newcomers. It is not uncommon for new superintendents, and even experienced ones, to call a valued peer and/or professor to discuss a difficult situation or seek some advice regarding an existing challenge. Often, then, it is this discussion or advice that significantly influences the superintendent's behavior in a particular situation or challenge.

Role modeling is another socialization practice that greatly affects the behavior of superintendents, particularly new ones. These individuals have invested several years in education prior to assuming a superintendency. They have been teachers, building-level administrators, and frequently, central office administrators. In each of these roles, and particularly in their administrative capacities, they have observed one or more superintendents in action. They noted how those superintendents worked with their boards, unions, parents, and communities. They observed their communication skills and leadership styles. These observations were mentally noted and recalled later for application to their own situations. It should be noted that modeled learning can also give one clues on how *not* to act. In other words, while some learning is observed, noted, and emulated, other learning is observed, noted, and discarded. In the latter case, the behavior of the model is considered to be inappropriate for the situation or role. For example, an aspiring or new superintendent may have observed a superintendent who had poor relationships with the community or board and noted that such behavior was not conducive to being an effective chief administrator. Or perhaps the model superintendent exhibited an authoritarian leadership style in inappropriate situations. Again, the observer noted that such behavior was not suitable.

## ACCESS TO THE SUPERINTENDENCY

After preparing oneself for the superintendency and becoming certified, how does one get in the right position to receive consideration for the real thing? The significant others that one is able to call on at this point become very important. For instance, the professors one had in the graduate administration program, the superintendent under whom one completed an internship, and one's mentor, if such a person exists, are often the individuals who can open the doors to a superintendency and who are frequently called upon for recommendations.

Janice Maienza studied some of the characteristics of access to the superintendency and used Kanter's structural elements of an organization as her focus. Those elements according to Maienza (1986) are:

> Opportunity . . . the state of being in a place where one can be noticed by others in the organization . . . Power . . . the ability to gather resources, to reallocate and use those resources effectively, and get things done . . . Relative Representation . . . the degree to which one individual is represented in the organization by others like him or herself. Persons represented in the organization by high relative numbers are a part of the "in" group. (p. 61)

Opportunity translates into being visible to those in top positions in one's own system or another system and having one of those individuals act as a sponsor for career advancement. Power means that one should volunteer for and accept assignments that will demonstrate one's administrative knowledge and abilities. Relative representation means becoming an accepted member of the chief administrator's group.

Mentoring is an important part of opportunity. Many individuals, both men and women, move into the top position because of a mentor. A mentor is an influential person who helps one achieve his/her goals, which in this case is a superintendency. The mentor invites the protégé into the upper echelon world, introduces the person around, shares knowledge, offers criticism, sponsors the individual for important assignments or key positions, and most importantly imparts his/her blessing indicating that, This is my choice. Mentors frequently identify and nurture their own protégés, but it is not uncommon for protégés to seek out mentors. In the latter case, the person identifies what one needs to learn and a list of possible mentors who could assist in this learning. Then, the protégé seeks to become one of those individual's understudies. In doing this, it must be clearly understood that the foundations of mentoring are trust and sharing. The individuals involved must be willing to trust each other and share their knowledge and expertise.

## CONCLUDING COMMENT

The socialization of a superintendent begins prior to assuming the role and continues during the performance of the role. Individuals who anticipate seeking a superintendency, as well as those who are already practicing, should understand that their socialization does not stop. They must continue to seek new knowledge, develop new skills, and hone existing ones. The role expectations, their own as well as those with whom they interact, are often in the process of revision. New significant others enter their lives. All of these changing socialization components result in changed role performance.

## REFERENCES

Baldwin, A. (1969). "A Cognitive Theory of Socialization." In D. A. Goslin (Ed.), *Handbook of Socialization Theory and Research* (pp. 325-345). Chicago: Rand McNally & Company.

Bandura, A. (1977). *Social Learning Theory.* Englewood Cliffs: Prentice-Hall, Inc.

Berger, P. L. and T. Luckmann (1967). *The Social Construction of Reality.* Garden City: Anchor Books.

Brim, O. G. and S. Wheeler (1966). *Socialization After Childhood: Two Essays.* New York: John Wiley & Sons.

Clausen, J. A. (1968). "Socialization as a Concept and as a Field of Study." In J. A. Clausen (Ed.), *Socialization and Society* (pp.3-17). Boston: Little, Brown, & Company.

Greenfield, W. D. (1985). "The Moral Socialization of School Administrators: Informal Role Learning Outcomes." *Educational Administration Quarterly, 21*(4), 99-119.

Louis, M. R. (1980, June). "Surprise and Sense Making: What Newcomers Experience in Entering Unfamiliar Organizational Settings." *Administrative Science Quarterly, 25*, pp. 226-251.

Maienza, J. G. (1986). "The Superintendency: Characteristics of Access for Men and Women." *Educational Administration Quarterly, 22*(4), 61.

Mead, G. (1934). *Mind, Self, and Society.* Chicago: University of Chicago Press.

Phillips-Jones, L. (1982). *Mentors and Proteges.* New York: Arbor House.

Sarbin, T. R. and L. Allen (1968). "Role Theory." In G. Lindzey and E. Anderson (Eds.), *The Handbook of Social Psychology* (Vol. 1). Reading: Addison-Wesley Publishing Company.

Shapiro, E. C., F. P. Haseltine and M. P. Rowe (1978, Spring). "Moving Up: Role Models, Mentors, and the 'Patron System'." *Sloan Management Review*, pp. 51-58.

Spencer, M. and A. Inkeles (1976). *Foundations of Modern Sociology.* Englewood Cliffs: Prentice-Hall, Inc.

Wolcott, H. F. (1973). *The Man in the Principal's Office: An Ethnography.* New York: Rinehart & Winston.

# CHAPTER 19

# Obtaining a Superintendency

The last chapter addressed the things one does to prepare for a superintendency. This chapter discusses the process one must go through in obtaining one.

There are a number of good general publications available on such things as résumé writing, interviewing, and dressing for success, and there are also a number of good publications on the specific process of applying for a superintendency. As one prepares to apply for a superintendency, these publications should be read. This chapter is not an attempt to recreate these existing publications but rather to highlight specific pointers that may prove helpful in the application process and to identify pitfalls to avoid.

Before discussing the nitty-gritty of applying for a superintendency, it is necessary to emphasize that the most important thing one can do to posture oneself as a serious superintendency candidate is to do a good job in the position one currently occupies. One must make decisions that are appropriate for the current position and situation and not for how they might further one's superintendency aspirations. Decisions made for the wrong reasons generally are poor decisions. If one approaches each position as the most important thing in one's professional life at the time, the enthusiasm and dedication so engendered will be a great asset in climbing the organizational ladder. In the contemporary setting there is too much happening for anyone to attempt to use impact on career advancement as a factor in decision making.

While this chapter will probably be of the greatest help to an aspiring superintendent, it is surprising to note how often seasoned superintendents who are applying for another superintendency make the same mistakes. Thus, if one is a practicing superintendent but has not changed positions in several years, much of the material in the chapter will serve as helpful reminders.

## GETTING IN THE STARTING BLOCKS

It is necessary for the superintendent aspirant to sit down with his/her family and make some very basic decisions before completing the first application. Things such as the type of district and community in which the applicant and his/her family can function and live comfortably must be addressed. Professionally, if one has been an urban dweller all one's life, it will probably be very difficult to function effectively as a superintendent in a very rural setting, or vice versa. If both spouses are enthusiastic about a move and view it as a challenge, families can enjoy almost any situation; however, an unhappy spouse has caused more than one superintendent to make a move at a less than opportune time.

How geographically mobile is the family? It's easy in the excitement of contemplating a move for the spouses to agree that there will be no geographic restrictions, but when the aspirant is actually offered a position and moving becomes a hard reality, hesitations begin to mount. The children cry, it seems more necessary to remain close to elderly parents, the good times one has had in the area are recalled, etc. If one goes through the application process, is offered the superintendency, and then turns it down because the community is not appropriate or the family has balked at the move, it will be many years before this stigma is removed. Those who promote and screen individuals for superintendencies don't like to be embarrassed in this manner. It must be added that making a decision not to accept a superintendency for these reasons is not to be confused with legitimately refusing a position because of extenuating factors that surface during the interview process.

Once one has decided to *go for* a superintendency, there are several things that should be done. First, let others know that you are interested in making a move. These others could be college professors, associations and individuals who perform superintendent searches for school boards, college placement offices, professional friends, relatives, and one's current superintendent. A good lead can come from anywhere. As a word of caution, at times one must use discretion in informing one's current superintendent; however, fortunately most superintendents are anxious to help their subordinates advance. At any rate, before one is offered a superintendency,. the board will check with the current employer. Thus, it is only a matter of time until one informs his/her superintendent—not whether.

Start a placement file at a university placement office. If you already have one, make sure that it is current. Ask individuals who should know about your job performance to write recommendations for inclusion in your placement file.

A brief discussion relative to obtaining appropriate references is in order because obtaining references is ongoing throughout one's professional career. First, always extend the courtesy of asking an individual if it is okay to use him/her as a reference. Second, make it easy for an individual to complete a reference for you. Briefly, and in writing, describe the job for which you are applying and some suggestions as to what might be addressed in the reference. Provide the individual with a copy of your résumé and a stamped envelope appropriately addressed. Always waive your right of access to the reference. Any reference in which this right is not waived or any reference that the applicant provides is always suspect.

Periodically, significant others in your career retire or move to other jobs. Obtain references from these individuals for your university placement file at the time of their departure. This is true even though you are not on the job market at the time. Also, your university placement file should be reviewed periodically to be sure that it is current and that it reflects the type of position for which you are currently applying. Usually, university placement officers or professors are willing to do this for you. While they will not relate the contents of the recommendations in the file to you, they will suggest additional references that would be helpful and identify references that perhaps are dated or inappropriate.

A résumé needs to be developed and kept current. Most university placement offices offer excellent seminars on résumé writing. Take advantage of them. Not only do they provide some good advice, but they also offer the chance to have your résumé critiqued. This is extremely important even if you are an old hand at résumé writing, for it is seldom that suggestions cannot be made for improvements.

It is through your résumé that you will be judged first. Individuals screening candidates for a superintendency vacancy will be scanning the résumés of thirty to one hundred candidates. The word *scanning* is stressed. At the preliminary screening stage, the screeners will not be poring over the résumé of each applicant in great detail. Instead, they will be attempting, rather quickly, to identify candidates who look as if they deserve further consideration. Therefore, your résumé needs to be both scannable and complete. This is not an easy task, but it can be done.

A résumé must look neat and be consistent in style, and it should not have a cluttered appearance. Don't put as much information as possible on a legal size page and then reduce the page. The résumé must be pleasing to the eye. The different subdivisions in the résumé should be easy to identify, and the contents of the subdivisions should be chronologically arranged and easily read. One word of caution is in order. It is possible to make a résumé look too slick or too much like a Madison Avenue product, and this practice often leads to skepticism on the part of screeners and board members.

A résumé should be designed for a particular superintendency. This is particularly easy to accomplish in the current age of personal computers and word processors. Put first things first. That is, include the things that you believe will make you an attractive candidate early in the résumé. Items of lesser importance should be included toward the end of the résumé.

Be concise but complete with the contents of your résumé, and above all else, be honest. Don't make yourself out to be someone you are not. As a rule of thumb, do not include anything on a résumé you wouldn't want to be made public. On the other hand, do not leave gaps. For instance, in presenting your employment history, do not leave some years unaccounted for. This will raise questions as to what you were doing during this time and why the omission exists. In the final analysis, when one is done reviewing your résumé will s/he have a feeling for the real you?

## RUNNING THE RACE

Your preliminary work is completed and you have let it be known that you are in the market for a superintendency. It is spring and you are receiving notices of superintendent vacancies. You have already determined what type of system you wish to superintend, so you have been prioritizing the vacancies. Now you check out the top vacancies in a little more depth. Why is there a vacancy? Is the current superintendent retiring, moving to a bigger job, or has s/he been fired or asked to leave? What type of individual does the board seem to be seeking? Is it a split board? Usually answers can be obtained via informal contacts. If an individual or association is doing the initial screening for the board, either will be glad to respond to these types of questions.

You have selected your vacancies of preference and it is now time to make application. Follow the application instructions precisely. If special reference forms are provided, see that your references receive these forms. If a copy of your superintendent's certificate is to be included with the application, be sure that it is included.

Spend time completing the application. It is advisable to make a copy of the application form and complete a draft first. Honestly and forthrightly complete everything asked for on the application. Do not say "Please see résumé" or make such statements as "This is the ideal school system and community for me." If you are anxious and prepared to assume a superintendency, then this will suffice as a reason for applying. Make sure that the application form submitted is neatly typed; a handwritten application is always a no-no. There should be no grammatical and/or spelling errors and few typing corrections. If your typing skills are not good, get someone to do it for you.

Ask the university placement office to forward your file to the appropriate place. If you are serious about the position, do not leave it to the screeners to request your file from the placement office. *You* make sure that they have it. Make it easy for your credentials to be reviewed.

Now that your application packet has been completed, you are ready to compose a cover letter. Make it short. Do not try to restate the information contained in your résumé and application form in the cover letter. One page is usually sufficient. Include the purpose of the letter (you are applying for the superintendency), perhaps briefly call attention to a couple of your experiences that are particularly germane to this position; indicate that your placement file containing transcripts, certificates, etc. is being forwarded; provide both home and work telephone numbers; and indicate a willingness to provide any additional information that may be needed. Do not be arrogant by including a statement like, "I am the ideal person for your job." The cover letter should be on personal, not school stationery.

At this point, you have done about all you can do except wait. It is usually not appropriate at this time to have individuals calling the screeners on your behalf.

Boards usually will select from four to ten candidates to be interviewed. Round two of the application process begins. The second round becomes much more intense and personal. You are now going to have the opportunity to present yourself and your views to the board and other individuals such as citizens, teachers, classified personnel, and perhaps even students. This is possibly your first educational interview in which your fate will be determined by noneducators, the board. The questions and concerns will be different than those you experienced in interviews with educators for lesser positions. If possible, have some associates put you through a mock interview.

Now is the time to do your homework in earnest. Most boards at this time will send you a packet containing basic information on the school system and community. Study this information and request additional information if necessary. Learn the names and backgrounds of the board members. What are the current concerns and issues of importance to the board, community, teachers, etc? What is the history of the system? Often, a visit to the community prior to the interview is helpful. Perhaps a review of the board minutes for the past year will be revealing. Another source of information is the local newspaper. One can find current and back issues in the local library. This source can identify current and recurring challenges facing the system, and it can also identify the paper's position regarding the schools.

Anticipate interview questions. What are some ideas you have about the superintendency in general and about resolving certain district problems in specific. (Never be critical of current practices or individuals.) What are some of your strengths? What are some of your weaknesses, and how are you going to compensate for them? For instance, if you have never served as the spokesperson in negotiations, have you had other positive negotiating experiences and have there been other situations in which you have served as the spokesperson for a group? Why do you want the job? You will not anticipate all of the questions, but you should be able to anticipate a number of the important ones.

Be on time for the interview at all costs. Arrive in town in sufficient time prior to the interview so that you will have the opportunity to relax and collect your thoughts. Perhaps arriving the night before the interview will be helpful. Don't be hesitant about spending some of your own money for travel and lodging. Use some free time to talk with the local people about the system. They can provide one with views that may not otherwise be available.

Dress appropriately for the interview. This may go without saying, but a pair of shoes not shined or a rip in the seam of a suit coat can make a difference. You need every edge you can get.

During the interview, listen closely to the questions. Do not anticipate a question and start responding before the inquisitor has had a chance to completely voice his/her concern. After the question has been posed, look the individual in the eye and give your response. Respond to the question courteously, concisely, and with no more explanation than necessary. This means more than a yes-no response, but it does not mean entering into a long rambling dialogue. It is possible to talk yourself out of a job.

Anticipate some of the dynamics that may take place during the interview process. Sometimes one or two board members will dominate the interview, even to the extent of cutting short questions from one or more of the other board members. Remember that each board member has one vote. Therefore, you must tactfully return at some point to the concern of the less assertive board member(s). Some antagonistic questions may be posed, perhaps by design, to see how you react under pressure. Never under any circumstances lose your cool.

Some board members may get into byplay or chiding among themselves in an effort to ease the tension during a slow time in the interview, or perhaps before the interview starts. It is best not to become involved in interactions of this sort.

It is good to have several questions of your own to ask the board at an appropriate time, usually toward the end of the interview. Such questions as "What are you particularly proud of in your system?" "What are some of your aspirations for the school system?" or "What are you looking for in a superintendent?" are relevant types of questions. Materialistic types of questions, such as salary and fringe benefit concerns, are not appropriate at this time. If you have done your homework, you will know the general parameters the board is operating within with respect to these items. The second interview is the more appropriate time to discuss specific details of this nature.

Usually every candidate that the board has selected to interview is capable of effectively fulfilling the superintendency role. It often comes down to a chemistry that develops between the candidate and the board. Therefore, it is important that you present the real you. If a good chemistry develops under these circumstances and you are offered a job, you are off to a good start. If a false chemistry emanates because you have not presented the real you, relations with the board will probably deteriorate rather rapidly once you accept the job. There is no substitute for frankness and honesty. For a good relationship to exist, the board must not only feel good about you, but you must feel good about the board.

After the interview, a follow-up letter to the board members expressing your appreciation for the interview is appropriate. If additional material has been requested, supply it at this time. Beware of inundating the board with unsolicited materials and press clippings. Having others contact the board members on your behalf is done at times; however, this is risky business.

Usually boards do not ask more than three candidates back for a second interview. On occasion, only the candidate of their choice is invited back. Whatever the case, the second interview will be much more detailed and will revolve around specific board concerns for the district. The specifics of a contract will probably be discussed, and you most likely will be asked at the conclusion of the interview if you will accept the superintendency if offered. If at all possible, be prepared to give a direct response to this query.

Probably before you are offered the position, some or all of the board members will want to visit your current place of employment. Be as helpful as possible in providing a place for them to hold meetings. Arrange meeting schedules if they so request.

If the board visits the home turf of more than one finalist, this practice can possibly pose a problem, for there will be only one winner. Questions of competence and dedication may be raised within the system of the individual who was not selected. This is particularly true for practicing superintendents. The visiting board should extend the courtesy of asking permission from the finalist to visit his/her school and community. However, if board visitation is a problem, it probably should have been addressed during the second interview. It is hoped that in the future more boards will visit only the community of their selected candidate.

## CROSSING THE FINISH LINE

You have just received a call and been offered a superintendency. At this point you will talk contract in earnest with the board. You should know what the general salaries and fringe benefits are for similar districts in the area, and what you are willing to accept. At this point, most boards will want to bring closure rather quickly to the selection process. This is a delicate time, for you and the board are both on a high. Serious negotiating can cool this relationship; however, it is important to get things in writing at this time. In addition to salary and fringe benefits, such things as professional leave, the process to be used in your evaluation, and the conditions under which you may be released from your contract (either at your request or the board's) should be spelled out. It may be necessary to consult an attorney in the process, but it is not recommended, however, that your attorney and the board's attorney do the negotiating on behalf of you and the board. Problems can easily develop under this scenario.

Obtaining one's first superintendency is difficult. Therefore, a beginning superintendent is not in a good bargaining position. It is suggested that attempting to get a number of concessions from the board during contract negotiations can be counterproductive. At this point, the board is somewhat at a disadvantage for the word has probably gotten out that you have been offered the position. If they feel that you are taking undue advantage of this situation, they will have the last laugh. On the other hand, if you accept a reasonable offer and do a good job, it is hypothesized that you will be rewarded accordingly in future years.

One last comment is in order as you cross the finish line and proceed to your new job. Leave your present job and district with good feelings. Resist the temptation to get in some parting shots at your former boss, board, or whomever. Leave with dignity and class.

## OBTAINING A SUPERINTENDENCY AFTER BEING FIRED

An unfortunate fact of life is that superintendents do get fired. The dismissal does not always show up as a firing in the local newspaper. One may resign under pressure of nonrenewal, one's contract may be bought out, or one may obtain another position before the hangman performs his dastardly deed. Whatever the case, the local community and the general educational community usually know the real story.

On the positive side, being fired from a superintendency is not the professional kiss of death it was several years ago. In fact, fired superintendents represent a very capable and competent pool of superintendency applicants.

There are professionally viable and acceptable reasons that superintendents get fired. For instance, a superintendent may be hired by a school board having one or more of the following as high priority items: the strengthening of staff evaluation procedures, passing a levy, consolidating or closing schools, etc. These are all tough issues. In accomplishing any one of them, a significant segment of the community can be alienated. If the alienation is great enough, new board members are elected, often with the stated goal of changing superintendents. As another example, some board members at times may get inappropriately involved in personnel selection. The superintendent may have to say no at times to such unwarranted board member involvement. Even if done tastefully and tactfully, this action can take its toll on board member support. At other times, such as after a strike, the superintendent is the scapegoat as the community and board look for someone to bear the brunt of the unpleasantness. On other occasions, the chemistry between the board and superintendent just isn't good. This generally does not happen overnight, but gradually escalates over time. Nevertheless, it is a situation that can lead to dismissal.

As illustrated above, the key becomes *why* was one fired. The examples represent professional superintendency hazards that one cannot always avoid. On the other hand, if the dismissal was for such things as the inappropriate use of public funds or grossly inappropriate personal conduct, it will probably be very difficult if not impossible to obtain a superintendency, which is as it should be.

The information contained in the preceding three sections of this chapter also applies to fired superintendents. However, due to the special circumstances, there are some additional considerations that former superintendents in this category need to take into account.

Being dismissed from a prestigious, high-visibility position is a humbling experience. This is particularly true if this is the first major setback in an otherwise successful personal and professional life. It can give even the most confident individual feelings of self-doubt and personal inadequacy. It will raise feelings of bitterness, vindictiveness, anger, and spite. In short, it places one in a very tense and unnatural mental state. Thus, the first thing to do is nothing. Don't say or do things that will be regretted later. Don't overreact. Things generally are not as bad as they seem. You are not the first nor will you be the last superintendent to be in this predicament. Take time to allow things to settle into their proper perspective. Talk with trusted friends. Attempt to view the situation as an unpleasant professional interlude that can and will be positively overcome.

In applying for another job, be honest. Don't pretend the dismissal, or in the case of a forced resignation, a pending dismissal didn't exist or worse yet, don't be misleading about the situation. Probably nothing turns off superintendency screeners or boards quicker than the thought that they are being misled.

Talk with screeners, professional friends, and personnel in the state superintendent and school board associations about your situation. This does two things. It makes them aware of your situation, and it helps make them a party to resolving it.

From your discussions, form a plan for honestly addressing the situation as you apply for superintendencies. Sometimes, a separate letter for inclusion in the application file is appropriate. This is particularly true if one has officially been relieved of duties or is currently employed in a lesser position than a superintendency. Also, consider how one will respond to probing questions during an interview situation.

Whatever your approach to addressing the situation, do not be negative toward the board that dismissed you. Board members relate to other board members. Recognize that a problem did exist, indicate why you believe it existed, and then go on to point out the many positive things that you and the board accomplished together. Your goal is to show that you can work effectively with your boss, in this case a board of education.

One last bit of advice is that every situation can be a learning situation. Reflect on your past experiences. What can you learn from them? What can or would you do differently? Doing this reflective thinking does not mean that you are accepting personal blame for the problems that led to your dismissal. Rather, it is an attempt to identify ways in which you can be a more effective educational leader in the future.

# CHAPTER 20

# After the Superintendency, What?

Superintendents are a part of the nationwide trend to retire at earlier ages. In a number of states, superintendents are qualifying for retirement in their early fifties. With the advent of early retirement incentive plans being adopted by some boards, at times the option to retire presents itself with very little advance notification. Although being eligible for retirement does not mean one has to retire, more and more superintendents are opting for the retirement option.

Unfortunately, retirement is about the only professionally and economically acceptable alternative to the superintendency. Unlike higher education where returning to professoring from an administrative post is a professionally and financially feasible alternative, returning to teaching from the superintendency in the public schools is not a viable option. Thus, retirement in many instances serves as an escape from the incessant rigors of the superintendency. Many, if not most, superintendents do not really wish to retire. Instead, they are using retirement as an avenue to career change.

Probably the most common error in making a career change is a lack of proper planning prior to making the change. Superintendents are busy people, and this planning process is something that can be easily postponed. Also, superintendents get used to being the center of attention. To many, it is inconceivable that their expertise would not be in great demand when they retire. Thus, it comes as a big surprise when upon retirement, the telephone in fact does not ring off the hook with people and organizations vying for their services. This silence serves as a rude awakening to say the least.

Therefore, how should one plan to exit the superintendency when one really doesn't want to retire? First one should begin thinking, talking, reading, and asking questions about making a career change from two to five years before one anticipates making such a change. In fact, no time is too early to begin. It can be a fun and exciting process for the entire family if it is done when not under pressure to make a decision.

Such questions as "How much money must one make? If one had one's druthers, what would one really like to do? Does one really want to return to teaching or would one rather be a travel agent? Has one always wanted to have a business of one's own?" etc. need to be addressed. There are books and seminars on these topics. Take advantage of them.

Look upon the planning process as an opportunity to stretch horizons and use imagination; it doesn't cost anything to daydream. Perhaps the financial base provided by retirement income will enable one to do something one has always dreamed about. One individual went to a Caribbean island ten years ago and started a charter boat service to explore coral reefs. Perhaps this example is a more esoteric undertaking than you wish to consider; however, the point is, look at alternatives. Don't approach career change with blinders.

If geographic relocation is a consideration, begin to take vacations in the desired area during different seasons of the year. Is this really a desirable location in which to reside the year around?

Once one has begun to narrow the responses to the questions above, an assessment of personal strengths and skills must be performed. Help may be needed in conducting such a task because most individuals possess much more expertise than they give themselves credit. (This is particularly true of superintendents.) Via the vast array of experiences one has had over the years as a teacher and administrator, many technical and human skills have been acquired. Once these skills have been identified, there is probably no career change area to which they cannot be creatively and innovatively applied. Thus, with proper planning the number of career change opportunities is limited only by one's imagination. In reality, the superintendency, in conjunction with the path one has followed to become a superintendent, prepares one exceptionally well for life after the superintendency.

While it is impossible to identify all the possible alternatives for career change, there are four general areas that can be explored. Each of these areas will be discussed briefly in the next sections.

## PRIVATE SECTOR—NONEDUCATION RELATED

This is a vast arena with unlimited options. However, it is the area with which superintendents are usually the most unfamiliar because it is the farthest removed from education. Thus, it is the area that probably presents the greatest challenge. New networks will have to be developed, and supply-and-demand thinking must be honed.

The human skills one has developed over the years can be put to good use in the private sector. For instance, most of the larger companies have public, customer, and/or community relations departments. In addition, one may have developed some specialized technical skills, such as in personnel management, which will serve one in good stead.

One may wish to strike out on one's own. Most small businesses fail due to a lack of management skills on the part of the owners. The superintendency experience should put one a step up in this area and increase the probability of success.

## PRIVATE SECTOR—EDUCATION RELATED

The private sector spends more money on education than the federal government. With the increased emphasis on well-trained employees who like what they are doing and where they are doing it, human resource management is going to be an exciting area in the years ahead. Training and development activities, writing training manuals, developing innovative fringe benefit packages, and devising innovative ways in which employees can become involved in decision making are but a few of the areas that are receiving, and will continue to receive, attention. Former superintendents are uniquely qualified for many of the activities that take place in this area. However, efforts must be put forth to make the appropriate contacts because there is considerable competition from organizational development specialists.

Perhaps during one's tenure in education some personnel or organizational needs that are going unfulfilled have been identified. For instance, one individual is doing very well selling supplemental retirement insurance. Perhaps there is a new product on the market that fills a void and would be exciting to sell. Thus, there are ways in which one can take advantage of educational contacts to help market products or services that will benefit either educational personnel directly or school systems in general.

## PUBLIC SERVICE AGENCIES

There are a host of public service agencies that are constantly looking for innovative leaders who can provide services on a limited budget. This in itself should make superintendents prime candidates. However, there is more. Most of these agencies have volunteer citizen boards that are somewhat akin to school boards. Fund-raising usually is a primary agency activity. While the agency fund-raising schemes differ from school fund-raising efforts, the basic job of convincing individuals that the organization is worthy of financial support is the same. And in the final analysis, these agencies are service agencies like schools. If one really enjoys providing leadership to a public service organization but would like to do so in a less fishbowl-like atmosphere than is possible in the superintendency, then seeking employment with a public service agency could be a very attractive option.

## EDUCATION

Many retired superintendents acquire other positions that are in the mainstream of education. This is good if one does this by choice and not by default. To accept such a position because little thought had been given to the direction a career change would take and this was the only job available does neither oneself nor education a favor.

In most teacher retirement systems there are restrictions as to how much one can work and/or how much one can earn in public education and still maintain retirement status. Be sure to thoroughly check out the regulations in your particular retirement system.

Some superintendents retire to a superintendency in another state. Thus, really only the location of their work changes. This move is usually made for monetary reasons, i.e., retirement income plus the salary from the new superintendency is much more than just superintendency income.

There is an increasing opportunity for employment as an interim superintendent. Former superintendents are employed for a period of up to one year to fill the void while a board is searching for a new superintendent. This same concept applies to other administrative positions. In fact, some retired superintendents have formed consulting firms to provide interim administrators to school systems.

A number of retired superintendents remain in education at the K-12 level by accepting employment in private schools. This often is a good situation for both the individual and the school. The school gets a quality individual at a salary that is usually considerably less than the going market rate. The individual can negotiate the terms of his/her contract to suit his/her personal desires, and the pressures and pace are less than those experienced in the superintendency.

Many superintendents desire a career change to the professorship at the university level, but full-time positions of this nature are very competitive. If one does desire to make such a move, one should begin planning early in one's career. For instance, publications are important in obtaining a professorship. Most practitioners have none, which puts them at a distinct disadvantage. Thus, it is important to write for publication along the way. There are many things going on in a school system that are worthy of publication; however, one must take the time to identify what they are and then must put forth the effort to reduce them to writing. Writing for publication is not an easy task. As such, it is easy to let other things take a higher priority. To guard against undue procrastination, set a goal of perhaps one published article a year.

If possible, teach a university course periodically. Do a good job of teaching the course. Do the necessary homework. A good course is much more than the relating of war stories. Teach as one would want one's teachers to teach. Perhaps help conduct workshops. These are more concentrated than courses, often lasting only one week or several weekends. Serve on university committees. This not only gets you in contact with appropriate people but it also enables you to get a glimpse of how universities operate. And of course, above all, be a good superintendent. Universities don't employ poor superintendents.

Also, universities expect that one's knowledge of administrative theory is current. A degree obtained ten or twenty years ago without evidence of periodic updating won't be acceptable.

There are limited opportunities for employment with professional associations. In addition to executive directorships, there are positions as field representatives, lobbyists, etc. These jobs are not as plentiful as other types of positions, but they can be personally re- warding as well as providing a service to the education profession.

Some superintendents opt for the consulting route. This is a very demanding and difficult route. The competition is keen whether employment is taken with an established consulting firm or whether one strikes out on one's own. Usually one must possess a recognized area of expertise to *make it* in the consulting field. Unless one is employed by an established firm that trains individuals for their specific needs, it is extremely difficult to be a viable consultant on a learn-as-you-go basis. Consulting is a field that requires much thinking and planning prior to retirement.

In conclusion, the thrust of this chapter has been to stress the importance of planning for a career change. Place yourself in a marketable position. Take control of your future. Be able to say more than "We're going to travel for several months, and then we'll begin to make plans for the future."

# PART FOUR

# Health, Happiness, and the Superintendency

This final subdivision of the book addresses the *private life* of a superintendent. The topic was deemed worthy of a separate subdivision, for the private life of a superintendent is really not so private. The superintendent and his/her family are exposed to constant scrutiny and pressures that are different from those experienced by anyone else in the school system or community, including the mayor.

The prototype individual aspiring to a superintendency has worked full-time while completing the graduate course work required to receive administrative certification. The aspirant usually has worked as a building-level administrator and probably as a central office administrator. Thus, the aspirant and the aspirant's family are no strangers to long hours of hard work and sacrifice. The aspirant also has been exposed to some intrusions into his/her private life.

While the above experiences are a necessary part of the superintendency preparation process, they do not adequately prepare one for the continuous and intense public scrutiny that accompanies the superintendency. Thus, this subdivision identifies some of the intrusions into the private life of the superintendent and his/her family and suggests some coping strategies.

# CHAPTER 21

# Life in the Fishbowl

When one accepts a superintendency s/he moves into the fishbowl. One now becomes a big fish in a small pond. This is particularly true in a smaller district where one usually obtains his/her first superintendency. Having one's every action closely scrutinized and constantly being the center of attention can be very exciting and exhilarating at times, but it can also be frustrating and stressful for the entire family at other times.

Expectations of a superintendent vary both by region of the country and community. However, some commonalties can be identified that are present in most, if not all, situations and must be addressed. They go with the territory. As such, it is necessary to be aware of these intrusions into one's private life and to do some thinking about how one will respond to them.

The chapter is divided into three sections. The first section addresses the personal demands placed on a superintendent. The second discusses the impact on the family, and the third identifies the unique aspects of being a single superintendent.

## PERSONAL DEMANDS

In reality, the superintendent is on duty twenty-four hours a day, seven days a week, as long as s/he is within the district. The super-

Mr. Roger Stiller provided the basic material for the first two sections of this chapter. Mr. Stiller is superintendent of the Columbiana Schools in Ohio. He has had two children attend school systems in which he has been a superintendent or central office administrator.

Ms. Linda Huntley and Mr. Stanley Heffner provided the basic material on the single superintendent. Ms. Huntley and Mr. Heffner are superintendents of the Midview and Madison Schools respectively in Ohio.

intendent is always viewed as representing the school system, and as such, is held to a higher standard of conduct than others within the community. Perhaps this is a carryover from the days when female teachers were not to be married.

The community expectations are such that the superintendent generally is not expected to play tennis at a public court on Saturday morning unshaven, without a shirt on and probably should not stop at the local pub for a beer on the way home. Appropriate tennis attire is expected, and perhaps a drink at one of the area's choice restaurants is acceptable. A Saturday evening at a local night club could be suspect, and under no circumstances will driving while intoxicated (DWI) be tolerated. An innocent stop at the hardware store on Saturday morning or a quiet time at church on Sunday morning can turn into a forum on the shortcomings of the football coach or on financial planning. Examples of intrusions could continue, but suffice it to say, that while the superintendent is in town there is no *time-out* period and can even be extended to one's home where the phone can be the conveyer of intrusions. This type of intrusion, however, can be controlled to a greater degree than the face-to-face interactions while out in the community. An unlisted number is not recommended, but it is an alternative.

Selecting a bank, an insurance agent, a real estate agent, buying a car, and shopping are subject to scrutiny and possible criticism if *inappropriate* choices are made. It is an individual preference as to how political one wants to be and should be in making these selections. However, it would be an unwise superintendent who would not at least take into account the potential personal and professional ramifications that could ensue by going against the tide. Perhaps no one will say a word about the selections, but five months later one may be scratching one's head on why a couple of the power brokers in town are remaining silent on the upcoming school levy.

In many communities, one should have a good reason for going outside the community to make a major purchase, such as a car. Whenever possible, local businesses that support the schools should be given consideration, even at a slight cost to the buyer, the superintendent. An extra dollar spent locally may return dividends in a variety of ways in the future.

Usually the superintendent is expected to join and participate in service organizations and serve on community boards. These may be things that the superintendent would do anyway, but to be expected to do them as a condition of employment tends to diminish one's personal enthusiasm for them at times. In addition to participating in such organizations, there also may be some additional unwritten expectations as to which organizations should be selected for membership and participation. These expectations change over time, but if the superintendent of the district has always been a member of Rotary, Lions, or Kiwanis it would be prudent to weigh the pros and cons of changing this pattern before making a decision. Incidentally, many of these avenues used to be closed to females. Recent years have seen a change in this area, and today, females are eligible for membership in most of the service organizations.

If in doubt as to what is acceptable or what would be appropriate in a community, seek advice from several trusted friends and board members. Combine their advice with past history and make a decision accordingly. Perhaps the community is ready to accept a change. However, if there is some doubt as to the appropriateness of a choice, the adage that discretion is the better part of valor probably offers some good advice.

Finally, the selection of a community in which one feels comfortable is the real key. If an individual feels that the mores of a particular community will be unduly restrictive, then another superintendency should be sought. One's personal unhappiness or uncomfortableness within a community is very difficult to conceal for long. Because the schools are really their schools, citizens tend not to want an individual leading their school system and influencing their children who does not share their values, and it is difficult to fault this thinking.

## FAMILY IMPACT

A good place to start the family impact section is with a continuation of the preceding section, i.e., moving into a community. With greater frequency, school boards are requiring their superintendents to live within their respective communities. Rightly or wrongly, many boards feel that it is not possible for the superintendent to really be a part of the community and have a *feel* for it unless s/he resides in it. Also, they believe a credibility gap exists for the superintendent if s/he does not pay property taxes in the district or if one's children do not attend school within the district.

If one is serious about obtaining a superintendency, one can count on being questioned during the interview process relative to one's thoughts on moving into the community. Therefore, moving should be thoroughly discussed and decisions should be reached with the family prior to seeking a superintendency. Moving becomes a particularly important issue if one's spouse also happens to be a professional with limited mobility. Children can also raise some rather strenuous objections at the thought of leaving their friends. However, unless there are extenuating circumstances, such as having a child who is entering the senior year in high school, children seem to adjust nicely. This is particularly true if the parents are positive and excited about moving to the new community. Nonetheless, while in the midst of the newness and excitement of getting established in a new job and town, one should not forget to take time to stay in touch with their children's feelings and experiences.

If one is successful in the superintendency, one will likely move three or four times during one's superintendency career. Thus, it is imperative that the moving issue be laid to rest at the onset of one's venture into the superintendency.

Once a decision has been made that the family will move into the school district, other things come into play. Are there acceptable houses available in the new school district in a price range one can afford? In fact, will one even be comfortable living in the district? Often compromises must be made, particularly if one has become accustomed to residing in a more affluent suburban area.

Most school boards will reimburse for moving expenses and may provide living expenses for a short period of time while a residence within the district is being sought. However, unlike the private sector, most school districts do not help in the purchase of residences by providing low interest loans or by picking up the realtor fees.

A number of superintendents have experienced the joy of owning two homes at the same time. This can be particularly burdensome when the housing market is down. It is not unheard of for a superintendent to be a proud dual home owner for a year or more. Fortunately, some boards seem to be more seriously addressing this problem area and are identifying innovative ways to alleviate this issue. Hopefully, in the years ahead, this trend will continue. A relatively minor financial barrier of this nature (to the board that is) should not stand in the way of a board's ability to employ the best individual for the job.

The superintendency has an impact on school-age children. Sometimes the superintendent's children will be treated better than other children and sometimes they will be treated worse. The only certainty is that they will not be treated the same as other children. In this respect, being a superintendent's child is a little like being a child whose parent(s) are part of the clergy; one is held to different standards than other children.

On the negative side, it is unbelievable how nasty some teachers can treat the superintendent's child. For starters, remarks like "Why didn't your dad/mother close school today?" "Tell your dad/mother that if s/he would give us more money for supplies we could do a better job," and "Your dad/mother wouldn't want you to act like this" are not that uncommon. It escalates from here. In the aftermath of a strike or if a teacher has just been nonrenewed, remarks and actions can get a little wild.

Children can be very hard on other children. If the superintendent's child receives an award or is a starter on the basketball team, allegations will be made by some that the superintendent was an influencing factor, and the recognition was not deserved on its own merits.

At times, the child will hear some very disparaging remarks made about his/her parent. Often these remarks will be overheard as opposed to being directed to the child. They hurt nonetheless.

It is important that parents keep an eye on their children for telltale signs that being the superintendent's child might be taking an undue toll. However, it also is important not to overreact. Some children handle being the superintendent's child very nicely. Others are more sensitive and are bothered by the remarks and actions of others. The parents need to help the children understand why they are being treated differently and encourage them to take things in stride. They should be encouraged to vent their anger and frustrations in family discussions. Fortunately, most superintendent's children survive this period in their lives rather well, and in fact in future years, are able to laugh about some of the things that occurred.

Being a superintendent's spouse is not easy either. The spouse is looked upon as an extension of the superintendent. It is difficult for the spouse to be viewed as a thinking individual with the right to have ideas different from the superintendent. As with the children, the spouse will be asked questions about which s/he has no knowledge and over which s/he has no control. What the spouse says and does will reflect on the superintendent. If the spouse makes a remark about the schools or about an individual, by the end of the day the remark will be attributed directly to the superintendent. Even if s/he has discussed a matter with the superintendent, confidence must be maintained on many issues.

Being the superintendent's spouse also carries certain social expectations. S/he may attend more ball games, concerts, and community functions than one thought existed. S/he will be expected to be a hostess/host on other occasions at functions involving the board and staff.

Perhaps the most difficult part of being the superintendent's spouse is biting one's lip while being a party to verbal and/or written criticism of one's spouse. This usually is more difficult than being personally criticized. One's first reaction is to speak out defensively. To respond in this way usually adds fuel to the fire and does little, if anything, to help the situation. As with the children, it is important to keep things in perspective. Enjoy the positive aspects of being in the fishbowl and minimize the negative.

## THE SINGLE SUPERINTENDENT

The single superintendent has some additional pressures by living in the fishbowl that are not normally experienced by his/her married counterparts. This is true even though the expectations individuals and communities have for the personal conduct of their leaders is changing. In most instances, it appears as if community leaders are being held to a lesser standard of personal conduct than they were in the past. Today, constituents seem to be more accepting of human frailties displayed by their leaders.

The superintendency has been affected by these changing values, but probably not as much as other public leadership positions. Many citizens still view the superintendent as one who ought to represent the traditional American value system, i.e., married with a family, church attender, active in community affairs, etc. Statistics on the personal characteristics of superintendents bear this out. For instance, the divorce rate of superintendents is considerably below the national average while church attendance and the percent of superintendents who are married are above the national average. Thus, the single superintendent has unique community pressures because s/he does not fit the norm.

It is possible to be a divorcee and be a superintendent; however, even though the national divorce rate is over 50 percent with no indications in sight that it will lessen, the divorced superintendent is often subject to a special type of scrutiny. Divorce is viewed as personal failure, and personal failure doesn't equate with professional competence in the public's mind. It also implies instability, while marriage implies stability and continuity. It raises the question that if one cannot get along with a spouse, does one also have generally poor interpersonal relations skills. It also raises a concern that the individual is so career oriented that traditional family values have taken a back seat. The bottom line with these types of concerns is that people wonder if an individual with this personal background is the appropriate individual to provide educational leadership for the community's youth.

If one has never been married, this raises questions such as what's wrong with him/her anyway? Why hasn't s/he gotten married? There is the underlying assumption that the individual is *strange*, maybe even a homosexual, if one hasn't found a spouse. In addition, the same concerns about interpersonal relations skills and professional versus family values with which the divorcee must contend also surface.

There is a concern on the part of some that if an individual doesn't have children of one's own, one cannot really understand children. The fact that over the years the superintendent aspirant has been in contact with many more children for greater periods of time than most parents does not substitute for the fact that one is not a parent. This outlook has an inherent assumption that certain insights relative to understanding children are reserved only for parents. Of course, no theory or research to date supports this view.

In some quarters, the question is raised whether a single individual can be a good and moral role model for kids. Hollywood's image of singles as swingers and rogues stirs fear in the hearts of the prudent. The fact that singles work as hard, have the same bills to pay, manage households, and live lifestyles comparable to their married counterparts is sometimes not given sufficient consideration.

Most of the social world for professionals is designed for couples. The superintendent without a spouse doesn't fit. For example, one does not fit nicely into a bridge club if one doesn't have a spouse to keep the numbers even, or one does not fit in with a group of couples on a football weekend at the local university if one is the only individual without a spouse. Attending a social function alone often makes others feel uncomfortable. They believe that the single individual feels lonely and/or embarrassed about the situation. The result is that the single individual does not receive an invite to the function again in the future. These types of exclusions limit the informal social and political networking important for success in the superintendency.

The social activities of single individuals tend to be more suspect than those of married individuals. For instance, a married superintendent takes a vacation in the Bahamas because s/he needs to spend time with the family, while the single superintendent does so for the purpose of partying in the sun. A married superintendent can entertain at will, while whispers will start if a particular car(s) is seen too often or too late at the residence of a single superintendent. A sort of chicken-before-the-egg mentality seems to exist that says it's okay to marry but not to date.

Unfortunately, it is still a reality that in many communities the single female superintendent comes under greater scrutiny than her male counterpart. In general, there is not much a single superintendent of either sex can do about the above concerns except to be aware that they exist and that one's actions will be scrutinized accordingly.

If one is leading a moral life, then one need not be unduly concerned about the talk of a few. For, no matter what one does, there will be some who will talk.

One's behavior over a period of time, perhaps several years, is the only way that concerns relative to the single superintendent will be allayed. In the process of allaying these concerns, one should enjoy the positive aspects of living in the fishbowl. It does give one the opportunity to be heard and to be influential. Use these opportunities to advantage and enjoy being *the* educational leader.

# CHAPTER 22

# Confronting the Stress Factor

## THE GNAWING GNATS

You have been in the middle of tough negotiations with the teachers for the past five weeks. At times, it seems as if progress is being made. However, during the last week the sessions have really bogged down. Salary and fringe benefits are the big issues. Just yesterday you received notice from the state department of education that your state funds would be somewhat less than anticipated this year and that no increases should be projected for next year. This really leaves you in a quandary as to where to go in negotiations. You are beginning to become extremely tired, both mentally and physically. The evening bargaining sessions on top of a full day at the office are taking their toll.

This morning as you sit in your office and spend a few minutes trying to plan your day, you let your mind wander from the ever-present negotiations for a few moments to some other concerns. The results of student achievement tests published each year by the state should be coming out any day now. You feel your system has done well this year, but that there is room for improvement. You know the inevitable comparisons by the media with other districts will be forthcoming. The football team is not having a particularly good season and a number of citizens are becoming increasingly more vocal in their comments relative to the football coach. In your opinion, this individual not only is a good coach, but also is a good teacher and works well with students. This situation, too, is beginning to make demands on your time. You have a grievance that is going to arbitration tomorrow. You feel very comfortable with your position on the issue, but you must spend several hours today making final preparations for the hearing. Several hours that don't fit easily into your schedule. Your eyes settle on your schedule of meetings for the day. You have a citizens' advisory committee meeting this morning, a Kiwanis presentation at noon, and a meeting with your curriculum committee meeting in the afternoon. You also have to put together an information letter for delivery to your board members by the end of the day. Your thoughts are interrupted by a ringing phone. A board member who has been concerned about the performance of a particular teacher is on the line. The teacher is tenured and you are doing everything you can do to address the situation, but the board member wants some immediate action.

After spending twenty minutes on the phone with the board member, you hang up and take a moment to collect your thoughts again. You suddenly realize that your stomach has had a constant knot in it for the past two weeks. You never seem to have a moment, either on the job or at home, when your mind is free of school-related matters. You observe that you have been constantly reacting to a myriad of concerns. You have not been able to slow down enough to do any thinking and planning relative to providing long-range leadership for your district. At this point in time, the job just is not very much fun.

This type of schedule and these types of concerns continue day after day. Notice that no one activity or concern is a particularly overwhelming problem in itself. A K.O. punch is not present, i.e., your contract is not in danger of being nonrenewed—not at this point in time at least. It is the *gnawing gnats* that do the damage, not the isolated big events. More specifically, the persistent and unrelenting pressure that comes with constantly being faced with the unexpected, attempting to provide consistent and proactive leadership for the district while at the same time trying to meet the often conflicting expectations of a half dozen client groups as well as the expectations of the board, and trying to juggle a budget that is stretched to the breaking point combine over an extended period of time to provide the basis for superintendent stress.

Now let us take a more specific look at this thing called stress, the study of which is a relatively recent phenomena. Around 1950, Hans Selye was the first person to become interested in performing stress-related research. From this beginning, the study of stress mushroomed until in the early 1980s approximately 10,000 articles a year were written on some form of stress. Currently, it is estimated that stress accounts for up to 80 percent of all illnesses. Often only the symptoms of stress such as a headache, fever, fatigue, etc. are treated by the medical profession.

The human body's stress mechanisms were acquired during man's early stages of development when immediate reactions were required to combat specific dangers or to fulfill very basic human needs. For this reason, the response patterns of the body's stress mechanisms have become known as the *fight* or *flight* syndrome.

In a brief period of time, civilization has developed to the point where most of us no longer have to face the daily physical confrontations that once were required if life was to be sustained. Today, stress is primarily mental. People do things that we wish they wouldn't do, and usually we have no specific and immediate recourse to remedy the situation. Instead, the situation remains within us and causes that gnawing uneasy feeling. The body is still trying to react with a *fight* or *flight* response, but it does not have a ready outlet for this internal reaction. Thus, the stress mechanisms turn their fury on our bodies. Stress, in one way or another, affects most of the systems and organs in our body without selectivity. This type of reaction is called a nonspecific response and can be produced by any agent that causes discord in an individual's mind; thus, stress is a very personal phenomenon. What is one person's meat will be another's poison.

Stress has been defined in the following ways:

1. The nonspecific response of the body to any demand
2. The body's physical, mental, and chemical reactions to circumstances that frighten, excite, confuse, or irritate
3. A psychological reaction which causes a physiological action
4. Any event in which environmental (external events) or internal demands (goals, values, commitments, tasks, etc.) tax or exceed the adaptive resources of an individual (psychological), social system or tissue system (physiological) (Lazarus and Launier, 1978).

Some of the common causes of distress (stressors) are as follows:

1. Frustration at one's work
2. Frustration in one's private life
3. Lack of motivation
4. Personality conflicts
5. Role conflicts
6. Time pressures
7. Career frustration
8. Lack of closure
9. Continued uncertainty and strangeness
10. Fatigue
11. Physical violence or threat of
12. Physical injury or threat of

Note that all but the last three stressors are mental and/or emotional in nature. Also, the expectation of a stressful event can be every bit as stressful as the event itself, i.e., a board meeting. Therefore, the perceptions or thoughts one has become very important.

It is of more than passing interest to note that many of the first nine stressors are very much a part of the superintendency for most individuals. Therefore, stress comes with the territory. In fact, in future years as education comes under greater scrutiny, finances continue to be a problem, more structural changes are required within the organization, greater emphasis is placed upon being the educational leader, and in all likelihood, fewer administrators will be employed to help with these increasing demands, the stress associated with the superintendency will continue to increase.


## THE GNATTING DANCE

The constant stirring and agitating of the ever-present swarming gnats identified earlier can cause the mind and body to react in ways that are detrimental to good health and to a productive and enjoyable life. The gnats have started to dance with joy for they know that your stomach is frequently in knots, that you wake up in the middle of the night for no apparent reason with that queasy feeling, and that your effectiveness has been lowered as a person and as a professional. Your body is being gradually torn asunder.

Let us look at some of the specifics that are fueling the *gnatting dance*. You have become impatient. You tend not to listen to the whole story in your meetings and conversations. You are making hasty and ill-advised decisions. In short, you are beginning to prove that impatience is probably the single most important factor leading to bad or marginal decisions. At the same time, you are becoming more irritable, causing communication problems with the board, staff, community, and family.

At work, your power of concentration has decreased. As a result, your incidence of mistakes has increased, and the completion of tasks started has decreased. Your already full schedule has been pushed to the breaking point because now it is taking you longer to complete tasks and to correct your mistakes. You're in a vicious circle. The added pressures of time and the inability to efficiently and effectively cope with the myriad of ever changing demands lead to still more stress. At the same time that the individual tasks of your job are becoming more troublesome, the *big picture* is also becoming muddled. Your perceptiveness has decreased. You are reading people and events less well. The art of administration is decreasing. You begin reacting to symptoms instead of searching for the real problems. Your alternative identification capabilities have also decreased. You are now operating with blinders on. Each problem becomes a crisis. The feeling that everyone and yes, that even includes your spouse and children, is working against you becomes more prevalent.

At the same time that your ability to deal with people and situations is decreasing, your body begins to sputter. Consider briefly some of the things that are occurring physiologically. The hypothalamus, which is a part of the brain immediately above the pituitary gland, senses that something is wrong. Your stomach begins to churn. At this moment, physiological changes over which you have no control begin to occur. The hypothalamus sends word to the pituitary that something is wrong. The pituitary in turn sends word on to the adrenal glands located just above the kidneys. The adrenal glands spring into action and secrete anti-inflammatory corticoids (ACs) into the bloodstream. These ACs influence connective tissue to inhibit inflammation. Thus, the immunological system of the body is impaired. When the ACs reach the liver, sometimes called the chemical factory of the body, the ACs are transformed into other types of corticoids that affect the body in various, sometimes detrimental, ways. The ACs arrive at the kidneys and through a complicated process, hypertension occurs. The blood vessels are constricted throughout the body. The heart is now pumping against greater resistance causing your blood pressure to rise, and your blood also thickens causing the heart to work even harder. In addition, the sugar level in the blood rises and the fatty deposits in the blood vessels (cholesterol and triglycerides) increase. The ACs have also reached the stomach where the digestive juices are very acidic. Selye (1976) found, quite by accident, that the inflammation on the inside of the stomach wall keeps the acidic digestive juices from eating through the stomach lining. The ACs reduce the inflammation of the stomach lining and thus permit the acidic digestive juices to begin to eat their way through the stomach wall. The result can be a peptic or gastric ulcer—the common *stress* ulcers.

The central nervous system is also affected. The spinal cord, brain stem, and thalamus are components of the central nervous system that can be affected. The ability of the body to coordinate the various functions of the nervous system becomes impaired.

The body can resist the above physiological idiosyncrasies for a prolonged period of time; however, it is only as strong as its weakest vital part. Selye (1976), in performing over 2,000 autopsies, claimed that he never saw an individual who truly died of old age, but that in every case, a weak part of the body gave out. This knowledge was not as important when the average life span was thirty-five years of age. Few, if any, individuals would argue that our ancestors were not under terrific stress with all the trials and tribulations they had to endure. However, the average life span was such that the weakest part of the body was not given the time to completely break down. With a doubling of the average life span to seventy plus years, the weakest part of the body now has ample opportunity to break down. Thus, stress-caused physical problems are increasing. It is evident that treating a kidney or liver problem is not getting at the likely culprit—stress.

It is interesting to note that the same physiological processes occur in eustress (elation and happiness) as in distress, but they don't have the same negative effects on the body. As yet, researchers are not completely able to explain this peculiar phenomenon.

## GNEUTRALIZING THE GNATS

We have learned of the deleterious effects stress can have on one's professional and personal life and on one's body. Now we are going to identify ways to *gneutralize* the gnats—to slow their antics down to the point where they are no longer harmful.

The objective in seeking to gneutralize distress is to identify ways to keep it within tolerable limits, not to eliminate it, because a life free of stress would be a boring and unproductive life. To this end, thirteen (a baker's dozen) specific considerations in seeking on-the-job relief from distress are presented.

1. *Work within reason.* Take breaks. It is possible to relax even when going between meetings. Think of some pleasant thoughts. Make yourself aware of the many positive things going on in your environment. Over the long haul, work reasonable working hours. Productivity is the proper measuring stick, not the number of hours worked. Take vacations. Even

short vacations can have wonderful rejuvenating effects. There will always be a reason to postpone a vacation. A vacation missed is gone forever.

2. *Learn to deal with anger.* At best, prevent anger, and at worst, don't let it linger with you. A negative and angry person is an unhappy person. You have a job to do. While at times anger can make the adrenaline flow and help you to rise to the occasion, more often than not it just makes your job more difficult and may even create more problems through spontaneous ill-advised comments and actions.

3. *Do not always take work home.* A briefcase sitting on the dining room table is a nagging reminder all evening of work you could be doing instead of watching the Monday night football game. The same briefcase left on your desk in the office will enable you some peace of mind while watching the game, for your work is no longer just a few steps away.

4. *Come to work rested and relaxed.* Get enough sleep. The specific amount differs for each individual. Get up early enough in the morning to allow ample time to complete your pre-work routine. Arrive at the office relaxed and in a good mood. To do otherwise means that you are starting the day in a hole, and you may not dig yourself out the rest of the day.

5. *Make a plan for the day.* Do not let the entire day just happen and dominate you. Bringing a situation under control is usually the only thing that needs to be done immediately. Don't be constantly fighting zero-hour deadlines.

6. *Break a big job into a series of small ones.* A systemwide curriculum review is a staggering task when looked at in its entirety. Establish a time line for the various components of the review process.

7. *Make lists.* Don't try to remember everything. Make a note and free your mind to concentrate on other more important things of the moment.

8. *When possible, do not arrange stressful activities for late in the day.* Once the anti-inflammatory corticoids are in your blood, they do not leave immediately. Thus, the reason you are not able to go to sleep until past midnight after a tough board meeting is stress related.

9. *Anticipate crisis situations.* Certain types of crisis situations

can be anticipated during the course of the year, i.e., trouble at athletic events. Do thinking and pre-planning on how you will deal with them. Do preventive planning.

10. *Practice selective thinking.* This is difficult, but it can be done. Don't let a problem that occurred Friday afternoon and which you cannot address until Monday morning ruin your weekend. Tune it out of your mind until perhaps Sunday evening.

11. *Arrange for time to be alone.* A few minutes of solitude can do wonders. Plan some time for yourself.

12. *Pursue an avocation.* Identify something that you enjoy doing that is totally unrelated to your professional life, i.e., jogging, tennis, photography, woodworking, recreational reading, etc. This enables you to relax and get your mind off of your problems, thus giving your body a much needed rest from the gnawing gnats.

13. *Keep your job and importance in perspective.* Do the best you can to make your school system the best that it can be. However, remember that the system was operating before your arrival on the scene and will continue to do so after you have departed in search of other mountains to climb (or retire).

In gneutralizing the gnats it is also necessary to give some attention to the physical needs of the body. Five such considerations follow.

1. *Maintain a proper diet.* The body, like any complex machine, must be properly maintained. Eat regularly and wisely.

2. *Exercise.* Choose your form of exercise, but choose it and do it. Program it into your daily and weekly calendar. Making plans to exercise with another individual can often provide the needed incentive to follow an exercise plan when other activities look more inviting or appear to be more pressing.

3. *Socialize to the extent that it is enjoyable.* It is impossible to be a super professional, parent, and spouse all at the same time—a truism that is difficult to accept. Which activities of yours, your kids, and your spouse are the most important ones? Set some priorities, which by the way, is very difficult to do, for you will have more high-priority obligations than you will adequately be able to fulfill.

4. *Avoid crutches.* Moderation or abstinence in such things as alcohol, overeating, smoking, prescribed drugs, etc. will pay

dividends. Beware of and be alert for unplanned changes in any of these things.

5. *Have periodic physical examinations.* Every finely tuned machine needs a periodic maintenance check. Your body is no exception. Be sure that a treadmill test is included as part of your examination.

One final comment on the stress-reducing activities identified in this section is in order. Have the perseverance and self-discipline to carry through on the activities upon which you embark. How often have you started a physical exercise program that ran its course in one month? A wise selection of and follow through on job-related and physical stress reducers will keep the gnats at bay.


## THE GNAT GNOCKOUT

At this point the coup de grace in the form of a gnat *gnockout* is applied. In the last section, the gnats were gneutralized, now they are going to be put into hibernation.

To apply the gnat gnockout, one must stand back and take stock of the important things in one's life and then assess one's daily decisions to see if one is really leading a life that coincides with one's espoused values. A good starting point is to list the five most important things in one's life in order of priority. Most lists will look something like the following:

1. Health
2. Family
3. Religion
4. Job
5. Avocation

Health is extremely important for it has been said that he who has health has hope, and he who has hope has everything. Most individuals will also list family and religion ahead of job. Even Vince Lombardi who is credited with saying during his heyday as head coach of the Green Bay Packers that, "Winning is not everything, it is the only thing," also stated emphatically many times that nothing was more important to him than his family and his religion. Thus, one's job is often listed as approximately fourth in order of importance. However, when one faces reality as to what actually takes priority on a daily basis and what takes a backseat, one's job often assumes the number one position. If this is the case, then one probably has some soul searching in the offing.

One of the things that all the major religions espouse is the need to go beyond oneself and to express care and concern for others. In fact, a number of studies have shown that some of the people who have the least distress are those who are helping other people. A study done by the sociology department of Duke University indicated that a significant factor in finding emotional and mental stability was the ability to find something bigger than oneself in which to believe. The study stated that self-centered, egotistical, materialistic people score the lowest in any test for measuring happiness. Thus, while the superintendency is fraught with stressors, it can also be used as a vehicle for relieving stress, for the essence of the superintendency is a dedication to helping others. The gnats must not be allowed to obscure this goal. The superintendent must believe that personal efforts on the job are making a difference in the lives of students.

As a final suggestion, when the day has been particularly troublesome, take a few minutes to read and reflect upon the following poem:

### THE VALUE OF A SMILE

It costs nothing, but it creates much good.

It enriches those who receive it without
impoverishing those who give it away.

No one is so rich that he can get along without it,
no one is too poor not to feel rich when receiving it.

It creates happiness in the home,
fosters goodwill in business,
and is the countersign of friends.

It is rest to the weary, daylight to the discouraged,
sunshine to the sad, and is nature's best antidote for trouble.

Yet it cannot be bought, begged, borrowed or stolen
for it is something of no earthly good to anyone
until it is given away willingly.

(Anonymous)

# REFERENCES

Lazarus, R. and R. Launier (1978). "Stress-Related Transactions Between Person and Environment." In *Perspectives in Interactional Psychology*. New York: Plenum Publishing Corp.

Selye, H. (1976). *The Stress of Life*. New York: McGraw-Hill Eook Co.

The old Indian adage that one cannot really know what another is experiencing until one has walked a mile in the other's moccasins is very apropos to the superintendency. One cannot know what it is to be a superintendent until one has been a superintendent. Even though the reading of this book has not enabled one to obtain the superintendency experience, it is hoped that the reading has given one a *feel* for the superintendency and the things that are important in serving as the educational leader of a school system.

Obtaining a *feel* for the superintendency is important. There are a number of things pertaining to the superintendency that can be studied and learned. Some of these are presented in the leadership subsections on the personal and professional competencies of a superintendent. However, such things as one's personal value system, the impact of one's personality on others, specific organizational history, the interpersonal dynamics at play in a given situation, and the domino effect generated throughout the organization caused by a given decision cannot be taught, for there are an infinite number of combinations possible in any given situation.

Over a period of years one mentally catalogs, sometimes unconsciously, many thousands of personal experiences. Intuition or the art of leadership is the result of this extended and continuous mental-cataloging process. When applied to the superintendency, this process constitutes a feel for the superintendency.

Decision making can serve as a specific example of the importance of a feel for the superintendency. Much time is spent in graduate preparation programs on the decision-making process. However, such important points as who should be involved in and responsible for the decision making and how and when the decision should be made rely greatly on one's feel for the situation.

How and when a decision should be implemented also relies greatly on one's feel for the situation. The best decision in the world is useless if significant others are not committed to work for its successful implementation.

How does one empower others to make decisions and still maintain organizational focus? As presented in the chapter on transformational leadership, there are steps that can be taken to help maintain the organizational focus. However, as position power is minimized in an empowering situation, the art of influencing and motivating others becomes extremely important.

Additional examples and prose could be put forth on the importance of a feel for the superintendency. However, suffice it to say that leadership in general and the superintendency in specific are both an art and a science. Therefore, one must obtain a superintendency before one can combine the art with the science.

The superintendency is more than a job. It is a position for one who is obsessed with the belief that one is embarked upon a very important mission. This individual has a burning vision of what this mission entails and what the outcomes should be. The enthusiasm and commitment that one displays while pursuing this vision become contagious throughout the organization. Mistakes and problems along the way are looked upon as temporary inconveniences that must be positively overcome so that one can continue pursuing the vision. The vision may be dimmed somewhat at times by the daily trials and tribulations inherent in the superintendency, but it is never lost.

Finally, the superintendency is a tough, time-consuming, and demanding job. However, in the words of one of our country's great leaders, Theodore Roosevelt:

> It is not the critic who counts; not the (person) who points out how the strong (person) stumbles, or where the doer of deeds could have done them better. The credit belongs to the (person) who is actually in the arena, whose face is marred by dust and sweat and blood; who strives valiantly; who errs, and comes short again and again, because there is no effort without error and shortcoming; but who knows the great enthusiasms, the great devotions; who spends himself/herself in a worthy cause; who at the best knows in the end the triumph of high achievement, and who at the worst, if he/she fails, at least fails while daring greatly, so that his/her place shall never be with those cold and timid souls who know neither victory nor defeat (Hart and Ferleger, 1989, p. 2).

If an individual is committed to the superintendency, s/he should pursue one with vigor and with the knowledge and belief that it is one of the most important ways in which humankind and this country can be served. In the words of Thomas Jefferson, "If a nation expects to be ignorant and free, in a state of civilization, it expects what never was and never will be" (Seldes, 1966, p. 367).

*Have Fun* — and — *Good Luck!!!*

## REFERENCES

Hart, A. B. and H. R. Ferleger (eds.) (1989). *Theodore Roosevelt Cyclopedia*. Westport, Connecticut: Meckler Corp.

Seldes, G. (1966). *The Great Quotations*. Secaucus, New Jersey: Castle Books.

# INDEX

*(continued)*